First World War
and Army of Occupation
War Diary
France, Belgium and Germany

59 DIVISION
176 Infantry Brigade
King's (Liverpool Regiment)
25th Battalion
5 May 1918 - 28 May 1919

WO95/3021/10

The Naval & Military Press Ltd
www.nmarchive.com
Published in association with The National Archives

Published by

The Naval & Military Press Ltd

Unit 10 Ridgewood Industrial Park,

Uckfield, East Sussex,

TN22 5QE England

Tel: +44 (0) 1825 749494

www.naval-military-press.com

www.nmarchive.com

This diary has been reprinted in facsimile from the original. Any imperfections are inevitably reproduced and the quality may fall short of modern type and cartographic standards.

© Crown Copyright
Images reproduced by permission of The National Archives, London, England, 2015.

Contents

Document type	Place/Title	Date From	Date To
Heading	WO95/3021/10		
Heading	59th Division 176th Infy Bde 25th Bn King's L'Pool Regt May 1918-May 1919 From U.K.		
War Diary	Cromer	05/05/1918	05/05/1918
War Diary	Dover	06/05/1918	06/05/1918
War Diary	Calais	07/05/1918	08/05/1918
War Diary	Bours	09/05/1918	09/05/1918
War Diary	Estree-Cauchie	10/05/1918	31/05/1918
Heading	War Diary of 25th G Bn Liverpool Regiment From 1st June 1918 To 30th June 1918		
War Diary	Estree Cauchie	01/06/1918	16/06/1918
War Diary	Laires	17/06/1918	30/06/1918
Heading	War Diary of 25th Bn Kings Liverpool Regiment From July 1st 1918 To July 31st 1918		
War Diary	Laires	01/07/1918	09/07/1918
War Diary	Hestrus	10/07/1918	23/07/1918
War Diary	Bertrencourt	24/07/1918	31/07/1918
Heading	War Diary of 25th Bn Kings Liverpool Regiments From August 1918 To Aug 31st 1918		
War Diary	Mercatel Sector	01/08/1918	03/08/1918
War Diary	Barley	04/08/1918	08/08/1918
War Diary	Mercatel Sector	09/08/1918	20/08/1918
War Diary	Bretencourt	21/08/1918	23/08/1918
War Diary	Saulty	24/08/1918	24/08/1918
War Diary	Bourecq	25/08/1918	26/08/1918
War Diary	Hamet Billets	27/06/1918	31/07/1918
War Diary	St Floris	31/08/1918	31/08/1918
Heading	War Diary of 25th Bn The Kings (Liverpool Regiment) From 1st Septr 1918 To 30th Septr 1918		
War Diary	St Floris	01/09/1918	03/09/1918
War Diary	Lestrum	03/09/1918	07/09/1918
War Diary	Pont Du Hem	08/09/1918	13/09/1918
War Diary	La Gorgue	14/09/1918	29/09/1918
War Diary	Harlech Castle	30/09/1918	30/09/1918
Miscellaneous	Addendum	05/09/1918	05/09/1918
Heading	War Diary of 25th Bn The Kings (Liverpool Regiment) From 1st Octr 1918 To 31st Octr 1918		
War Diary	Harlech Castle	01/10/1918	03/10/1918
War Diary	Au Nouveau Monde	04/10/1918	04/10/1918
War Diary	Erquinghem Switch	05/10/1918	06/10/1918
War Diary	La Vessee Post Sector	07/10/1918	16/10/1918
War Diary	Erquinghem	17/10/1918	17/10/1918
War Diary	Daisy Post	17/10/1918	18/10/1918
War Diary	St Andre	18/10/1918	18/10/1918
War Diary	Madeleine	18/10/1918	22/10/1918
War Diary	Toufflers	23/10/1918	31/10/1918
Miscellaneous	GA 490/4		
Heading	22 General Staff Circular No.13 Amendment No.1 File 41		
Miscellaneous	General Headquarters D.A.G 3rd Echelon	05/04/1918	05/04/1918

Miscellaneous	25th Bn "The King's" L'Pool Regt	29/10/1918	29/10/1918
Miscellaneous	59th Division G.S. 67/36	27/10/1918	27/10/1918
Miscellaneous	Ref 76 Inf Bde Order No.138	22/10/1918	22/10/1918
Miscellaneous			
Operation(al) Order(s)	76 Inf Bde Order No.138	22/10/1918	22/10/1918
Miscellaneous	Reference 176th Inf Bde Warning Order No.137	22/10/1918	22/10/1918
Miscellaneous	Divisional Commander	21/10/1918	21/10/1918
Miscellaneous	The command will pass from G.O.C.		
Miscellaneous	XI Corps G.S. 67/37	26/10/1918	26/10/1918
Miscellaneous	General Headquarters D.A.G 3rd Echelon	04/11/1918	04/11/1918
Miscellaneous	Fifth Army G.A. 490/14	25/10/1918	25/10/1918
Miscellaneous	To move at 1/2 Hours Notice from 10.00		
Miscellaneous	A Form Messages And Signals		
Miscellaneous	XI Corps General Staff	23/10/1918	23/10/1918
Miscellaneous	XI Corps G.S. 67/37	23/10/1918	23/10/1918
Miscellaneous	XI Corps G.S. 67/37 59th Div G.871	22/10/1918	22/10/1918
Miscellaneous	A Form Messages And Signals		
Miscellaneous	25th "King's" (Liverpool Regt.)	21/10/1918	21/10/1918
Miscellaneous	Circulation Slip	24/10/1918	24/10/1918
Miscellaneous	Fifth Army G.A. 490/14	25/10/1918	25/10/1918
Miscellaneous	XI Corps G.S. 67/37	23/10/1918	23/10/1918
Miscellaneous	XI Corps G.871	22/10/1918	22/10/1918
Heading	War Diary of 25th Bn The King's (Liverpool Regiment) From 1st Nov 1918 To 30th Nov 1918		
War Diary	Toufflers	01/11/1918	08/11/1918
War Diary	Chaos	08/11/1918	09/11/1918
War Diary	Goudiniere	09/11/1918	10/11/1918
War Diary	Velaines	10/11/1918	12/11/1918
War Diary	Goudiniere	12/11/1918	15/11/1918
War Diary	Willems	15/11/1918	16/11/1918
War Diary	Thumesnil	16/11/1918	30/11/1918
Heading	War Diary of 25th Bn The Kings (Liverpool Regiment) From Dec 1st 1918 To Dec 31st 1918		
War Diary	Thumesnil	01/12/1918	06/12/1918
War Diary	Verdrel	06/12/1918	16/12/1918
War Diary	Barlin	16/12/1918	31/12/1918
Miscellaneous	Instructions for Embussing	05/12/1918	05/12/1918
Miscellaneous	A Form Messages And Signals		
Miscellaneous	D 19		
Operation(al) Order(s)	176th Infantry Brigade Order No.144	04/12/1918	04/12/1918
Heading	War Diary of 25th Bn "The Kings" (Liverpool Regiment) From 1st January To January 31st 1919		
War Diary	Barlin	01/01/1919	16/01/1919
War Diary	St. Venant	16/01/1919	17/01/1919
War Diary	Wallon Capel	17/01/1919	30/01/1919
War Diary	Dunkirk	30/01/1919	31/01/1919
Heading	War Diary For February 1919 25th Battn The Kings L'pool Regt		
War Diary	Dunkirk	01/02/1919	28/02/1919
Heading	War Diary of 25th Kings Liverpool Regt From March 1st 1919 To March 31st 1919		
War Diary	Dunkirk	01/03/1919	27/03/1919
War Diary	Beaumarais	27/03/1919	31/03/1919
Heading	War Diary of 25th Bn Kings Liverpool Regt From 1st April 1919 To 30th April 1919		
War Diary	Beaumarais	01/04/1919	21/05/1919

War Diary	In Route For Marseille		22/05/1919	22/05/1919
War Diary	St. Germaine		23/05/1919	23/05/1919
War Diary	H.T. Malwa		29/05/1919	31/05/1919
War Diary	Marseilles		24/05/1919	28/05/1919

W0 95/30211

59TH DIVISION
176TH INFY BDE

25TH BN KING'S L'POOL REGT.
MAY 1918-MAY 1919.

FROM UK

TO EGYPT 1919 MAY
3(INDIAN) DIV 7 BDE

WAR DIARY or INTELLIGENCE SUMMARY

(Erase heading not required.)

25th Bn L'pool Regt
Vol 1

Place	Date	Hour	Summary of Events and Information	Remarks and references to Appendices
CROMER	5.5.18		The Battalion under the Command of Lt. Col. R. C. Kay left CROMER by train for DOVER, under orders to proceed to FRANCE. Strength 37 Officers 1062 other ranks. The Train proceeded by SOUTHAMPTON to CALAIS	
DOVER	6.5.18	9.30AM	The Battalion Transport arrived at DOVER, and marched to the VICTORIA BARRAGE Rest Camp.	
		5PM	Embarked on board S.S. ONWARD but owing to heavy fog he were unable to sail and so returned Spending the night at the Rest Camp close to DOVER HARBOUR Station	
CALAIS	7.5.18		The Battⁿ Re-embarked on the ONWARD in heavy rain, and crossed to CALAIS without mishap. After disentraining the Battalion proceeded to No 6 Rest Camp EAST; Weather heaving, improved.	
CALAIS	8.5.18		During the Day the Battalion was taken in small parties through Gas. Enemy Aeroplanes dropped numerous bombs round FONTINETTES Station during the night. None fell near the Rest Camp	
BOURS	9.5.18		Major W.M. HOPE, THE WELSH Regt. takes over Command of the Battalion at O.C. Kay proceeding to hospital Sick. The Battalion Entrained at FONTINETTES Station for BRYAS near St-POL. Detrainment took Place at BRYAS Station, and the Battalion marched to BOURS (about 4km) where billets were found for the Night	

WAR DIARY

INTELLIGENCE SUMMARY

Army Form C. 2118.

Place	Date	Hour	Summary of Events and Information	Remarks and references to Appendices
ESTRÉE-CAUCHIE	10.5.18		The Battalion proceeded to ESTRÉE-CAUCHIE by motor-lorries, where tents and bivouacs were drawn and a camp pitched just E. of MAISNIL BOUCHÉ.	Ref: sheet 36¢ 1/40,000
"	11.5.18		Remained in Camp all day till 5 P.M. when tents were struck and camp moved nearer to ESTRÉE-CAUCHIE in quarries W.3.c. Orders were received for Commencement of work on a G.H.Q. Defensive line called the B.B. line. Major WEST-BY (2nd in command), and 6 other ranks were evacuated to hospital sick.	
"	12.5.18		G.H.Q. information received that the Batt'y will become a unit of the 177th Brigade, 59th Division. Work commenced on the B.B. line's front line from W.4.A. 80.50. to Q.28.C. 15.90. weather fine. 1 other Rank sent to Batt'y Sick.	Ref: Sheet 36c S.E. 1/20,000
"	13.5.18 9.30 AM to 4.30 PM		Work continued on B.B. line. C and D Coys on a switch line which joins the front line at Q.33.C. 80.30. A and B Coys Coy on the front line and 28 other Ranks leave Batt'y Sick. Rain most of the day.	"
"	14.5.18 9.30AM to 4.30PM		Work continued of B.B. line. A and B Coys on the front line, and C and D Coys on a Reserve line from Q.32.d.90.40. to Q.27.c.35.85. 4 other Ranks to hospital sick. weather fine	"

WAR DIARY
or
INTELLIGENCE SUMMARY

Army Form C. 2118.

Place	Date	Hour	Summary of Events and Information	Remarks and references to Appendices
ESTRÉE-CAUCHIE	14.5.18.		Orders received regarding the allotment of the following sector of the B.B. line to be taken up by the Bn in case of a break through by the enemy:- W.3.c.90.30. (Ref sheet 36 d. S.E. 1/20000) to E.3.d.50.0. (Ref sheet 51 c. N.E. 1/20000)	
"	15.5.18.	9.30am 4.30pm	Work continued on front and Reserve lines, B.B. line. Weather very hot so that work was done with difficulty. Reconnaissance of the B.B. hits in case of a break through was made by C.O. and Company officers. Positions for Coy H.Q. and Platoon H.Q.s chosen. 2 other Ranks to Hospital sick.	
"	16.5.18.	"	A and B Coys continued on front line and C and D Coys on Reserve line. Weather still very hot. 4 other ranks to Hospital sick.	
"	17.5.18.	"	A and B Coys completed front line and C and D Coys continued on Reserve line. Very hot weather. B.G.C. 177th Bde inspected the Camp. 4 other ranks to Hospital sick.	
"	18.5.18.	" 12 Noon	A and B Coys worked on the switch line. C and D Coys continued work on the Reserve line. Camp and transport inspected by the D.A.D.M.S. and D.A.D.V.S., respectively. Weather continues to get hot. 1 other rank to hospital sick.	
"	19.5.18.	9 AM	Inspection of Camp by Commanding officer.	

WAR DIARY or INTELLIGENCE SUMMARY

Army Form C. 2118.

Place	Date	Hour	Summary of Events and Information	Remarks and references to Appendices
RUITZ (AVEHIE)	19.5.18 (cont)		Church Parade in Camp attended also by Cadres of the 2/Lincolns and No work on B.B. line done.	
"	20.5.18	5:30 A.M. to	Weather too hot for digging. Worked for digging stopped on account of heat. Worked on the Switch Line and C and D Coys completed their Reserve line B.G.C. 177th Brigade inspected the Battln at 12 hours training which 10 am started from this date. Twenty five men per Coy from	1 other rank Hospital Sick. A and B Coys.
"	6 P.M.			
"	21.5.18	5:30 P.M. 5:30 A.M. to 11:30 A.M.	A, B, and C Coys inoculated. Continuation of Ref. Stretchers Sick Hospital. All coys worked on the Switch Line. New hours for drills. Obtained successful as time work was gone and the men been fatigued.	R.J. Chest 36 L.S.E./2000m
"	22.5.18	1 P.M.	6.50 two tanks hit at CAUCOURT 1 other rank hospital sick Enemy aeroplanes dropped 8 bombs in and around MAISNIL BOUCHE. Causing alarm a very Casualties at the XVIII Corps Reinforcement Camp. one B/poster in all Ratn Coys Continue work on the Switch line. 40 O.Rs hospital sick Battn lines	" R/Shurd 36t S.E. 1/2000
"	23.5.18	7 P.M.	2 bombs dropped on (ANSIGNEOL); effects not known. Weather hot. Enemy aerial activity during the night but no bombs were dropped in this vicinity. Work continued on Switch line. Weather fine with very strong wind.	
			1 other rank Hospital Sick	

WAR DIARY
or
INTELLIGENCE SUMMARY.
(Erase heading not required.)

Army Form C. 2118.

Place	Date	Hour	Summary of Events and Information	Remarks and references to Appendices
FOSSE F - CAUCHIE	24.5.18	5.30am to 10.30pm	Work starts on a new trench adjoining Switch line at Q.33.d.30.80. Complete change of weather, - cold and heavy rain continuing. Transport inspected in the afternoon by O.C. No 3 Coy Divisional Train. Training for Coys from 5c - 6.P.M. 20 Other ranks to hospital sick.	Ref: Sheet 36c, S.E. 1/20000
"	25.5.18		All Coys continued Trg (Coy 3). Weather improved (slightly.) Training in efficiency.	Othermen shown marked improvement 4 Other ranks to hospital sick.
"	26.5.18	8.am to 1.pm	The Batt took up its post in the B.B. line for practice. Coys marched in S.B.R! for 1/2 hour on their way to take up their positions. The positions chosen by Platoons for Lewis Guns Sentries (were) in most cases lack of common sense. Volunteers C.O.E. service in afternoon. Capt MACLAREN attached to Tools near the butcher (?) in command. Lt BUHMAN attached Commander of S.C Coy. Capt C.F. (R.C.) attached to the Batt! 1 Other rank to hospital sick.	
"	27.5.18	12am to 11am	Digging continued in good weather. The (?) Training took place before S/c.B.P.M. 3 Other ranks to hospital sick	
"	28.5.18	6.30am to 11.30pm	Digging starts at 6.30 A.M. to prevent reveille being too early. 2 Other ranks to hospital sick.	

WAR DIARY
or
INTELLIGENCE SUMMARY
(Erase heading not required.)

Army Form C. 2118.

Place	Date	Hour	Summary of Events and Information	Remarks and references to Appendices
ESTRÉE - CAUCHIE	29.5.16	6.30	Digging commenced 6.30 a.m. 3 other ranks to hospital sick. 5 a.m. heavy weather fine	
	30.5.16	6.30	Digging commenced 6.30 a.m. En route to our Ref. 20.13 A 80 approx. Enemy aerial activity in the morning, four aeroplanes reported & two dropped. Afternoon 18 reported each wearing fire	
	31.5.16	6.30	Digging continued in same sector. Enemy aeroplanes in vicinity, anti-aircraft dropped shells, and to hospital sick. Strength of Battalion = 26 Officers including C.O. 9 & 3 other ranks including 1 O.R. attached, another casualties to the fire.	

L.S. John of 1st Rgt Lt.

Army Form C. 2118.

WAR DIARY
or
INTELLIGENCE SUMMARY.
(Erase heading not required.)

Confidential

Original War Diary
of
25th G. Bn. Liverpool Regiment

From 1st June 1918
to 30th June 1918

Army Form C. 2118.

WAR DIARY
or
INTELLIGENCE SUMMARY.
(Erase heading not required.)

2.5th Garrison Bn. Kings (Liverpool) Regt.

for the Month of June.

Instructions regarding War Diaries and Intelligence Summaries are contained in F. S. Regs., Part II. and the Staff Manual respectively. Title pages will be prepared in manuscript.

Place	Date	Hour	Summary of Events and Information	Remarks and references to Appendices
ESTREE- CAUCHIE	1.6.18	6.30 AM 10.30 PM	All Coys worked on the Savy sector of the B.B. line – W.8. Weather fine. 7 other ranks to hospital sick	R.h. Ret sheet
	2.6.18	8 AM	The Bn. went for a practice 8 miles route march – 11 other ranks fell out. Ranks were not worn. 2.0 hrs. talk at Concert in the afternoon. Weather fine	4 + S.E 1/2000 R.h.
	3.6.18		3 other ranks to hospital sick. All Coys (less 50 men for training as Lewis gunners) worked in W.8. and W.14. Weather colder but fine. 4 other ranks to hospital	" R.h.
"	4.6.18		Digging as usual. Weather fine. 3 other ranks to hospital sick	R.h.
	5.6.18		Digging in W.14. Divisional Concert Party (The Crumps) gave a performance in the evening to the men. 8 other ranks to hospital sick	R.h.
	6.6.18		Digging in W.20. 8 other ranks join Battn from the 27th Liverpools.	6 R.h.
	7.6.18		Digging in W.20, and W.27. Weather a little colder. 27 other ranks to hospital from the base. 2 other ranks to hospital sick.	R.h.
	8.6.18		Digging in W.27. Weather fine. 4 other ranks to hospital sick	8 R.h.
"	9.6.18	7.30 AM 11 AM	Battn took up practice position in the B.B. line in conjunction with the 177th Brigade.	R.h.

Army Form C. 2118.

WAR DIARY
or
INTELLIGENCE SUMMARY.
(Erase heading not required.)

Instructions regarding War Diaries and Intelligence Summaries are contained in F. S. Regs., Part II. and the Staff Manual respectively. Title pages will be prepared in manuscript.

Place	Date	Hour	Summary of Events and Information	Remarks and references to Appendices
FAREE-CROCHTE	9.6.18.		The Divisional Commander inspected the line. Slight rain in the evening. 2 other ranks to hospital sick.	F.P.L.
"	10.6.18		Digging on observation trench of B3 line infantry sector started in Wig. bands. 9 other ranks to hospital sick.	F.P.L. Report 4th l/200oy
"	11.6.18		Digging on observation trench continued. Weather fine. 8 other ranks to hospital sick	F.P.L.
	12.6.18.		Digging continued in W.15. Ground hard. Weather fine. 11 other ranks to hospital sick	F.P.L.
	13.6.18.		Digging continued in W.15. Seventy other ranks arrived as reinforcement from the Base. 5 other ranks to hospital sick.	F.P.L.
	14.6.18.		Digging continued in W.15. The draft (70 other ranks) inspected by the Commanding Officer. 2 other ranks to hospital sick. 1 officer of P.V.O. to be with orders received from 177th Brigade that the 10th Inst. would be the last day for digging in B.3. line	F.P.L.
	15.6.18. 7.30 PM		Digging area in W.15 completed. Weather fine. # It still rain to hospital sick. Orders received from Brigade for the Battalion to be prepared to move to RAINIER Parky about 10 P.M. the 16.3 inst. 2 cases being the P.V.O. which Appears to be assuming an epidemic	F.P.L.

2353 Wt. W2544/1454 700,000 5/15 D.D. & L. A.D.S.S. Forms/C. 2118.

Army Form C. 2118.

WAR DIARY
or
INTELLIGENCE SUMMARY.
(Erase heading not required.)

Instructions regarding War Diaries and Intelligence Summaries are contained in F.S. Regs., Part II. and the Staff Manual respectively. Title pages will be prepared in manuscript.

Place	Date	Hour	Summary of Events and Information	Remarks and references to Appendices
ESTREE-BLANCHE	11.6.18	4.11 am	Orders received from 177th Brigade that the Battalion would have to move by lorries to AIRE at 10 am.	Appx. H/11.6.18 Appx 3a/10.00 am
		7.15 am	As no buses met the unit at the above Rdv, orders received that the above would be postponed for 24 hours. Weather fine. 36 other ranks Hospital sick. 38 (including P.U.O. epidemic amongst men).	Appx
LAIRES	12.6.18	10 am	The Battalion entrained and proceeded to LAIRE. The Battalion becomes a unit of the 176th Infantry Brigade, 59th Division. 37 other ranks Hospital sick. 31 being P.U.O. epidemic.	Appx
"	18.6.18	9 am	Training started — Short route one each day. Weather fine. 33 other ranks P.U.O. epidemic. 37 to hospital sick	Appx
	19.6.18	12 noon 3 pm	The battn was inspected during the morning by Major General Stuart WORTLEY Commanding the 59th Division. Officers' Conference at 3.15 pm. Brigade Headquarters on country. This unit to go underfield training on account of flu epidemic. 54 other ranks Hospital sick, 54 being P.U.O. epidemic, including 2nd Lieutenants L.A. CLAYTON and T.G. MORTIMER. Light training carried out. 115 Cases Hospital, all P.U.O. cases.	Appx
	20.6.18 21.6.18		Continuation of light training. 144 cases Hospital, all P.U.O. cases including	Appx Appx

2353 Wt W3544/1454 700,000 5/15 D. D. & L. A.D.S.S. Forms/C. 2118.

Army Form C. 2118.

WAR DIARY
or
INTELLIGENCE SUMMARY.
(Erase heading not required.)

Instructions regarding War Diaries and Intelligence Summaries are contained in F. S. Regs., Part II. and the Staff Manual respectively. Title pages will be prepared in manuscript.

Place	Date	Hour	Summary of Events and Information	Remarks and references to Appendices
LAIRES	21/6/18 (cont)		Initiative. Capt: B. Hutton R.E., A/Capt: C.G. Bulman, Lieut: A.M. Ferguson, and 2nd Lieut: P.W. Price. Weather showery. 22 OR were hospital sick, all being P.U.O. including 2nd Lieut: T.E. GEDR Y.E.	F.P.H.
	22.6.18		Weather showery. 14 OR to Hospital, all being P.U.O. and including Capt C.F. DUNNE Chaplain Capt E.A. MOORE + 2/Lt G.H. BROOKER	F.P.H.
	23.6.18			F.P.H.
	24-6-19		Weather showery. Capt H.C. HANKINS 6th (GLAM) 13 N WELSH REGT Ft took duties of Adjutant having been appointed vice Capt E.A. MOORE Middlesex Regt who has been posted to the 13th MIDDLESEX Regt. 30 OR to Hospital all P.U.O cases, one of which was the R.S. Major also Lt H.A. WALKER, 2/Lt E.G. EVANS + 2/Lt F.W. NUNNELEY	F.P.H.
	25-6-18		Weather showery. 27 OR to Hospital and 2/Lts F.P. JOHN + T. ORMEROD + all P.U.O cases. 2/Lt T.G. MORTIMER having OR returned from Hosp+ Capt B. HUTTON, Capt C.G. BULMAN	F.P.H.
	26.6.18		Weather showery. 9 OR to Hospital, all P.U.O. cases. Twenty four OR's returned from Hosp.	F.P.H.
	27-6-19		Weather showery. 10 OR to Hospital all P.U.O. 24 OR returned	F.P.H.

2353 Wt. W2544/1454 700,000 5/15 D. D. & L. A.D.S.S. Forms/C. 2118.

Army Form C. 2118.

WAR DIARY
or
INTELLIGENCE SUMMARY.
(Erase heading not required.)

Instructions regarding War Diaries and Intelligence Summaries are contained in F. S. Regs., Part II. and the Staff Manual respectively. Title pages will be prepared in manuscript.

Place	Date	Hour	Summary of Events and Information	Remarks and references to Appendices
LAIRES	27-6-18		2nd Lt A.M. FERGUSSON & 2Lt T.E. GEORGE from Hospital	
	28-6-18		Weather fine. 3 OR to Hospital, all P.U.O and 19 OR returned from Hospital	
	29-6-18		Weather fine. 7 OR to Hospital & also OR returned	
	30-6-18		Weather fine. 3 OR to Hospital and Capt GWYNN 2/Lt FOXALL 2/Lt GWYNN R.F. GWINN, 2/Lt T.W. FOXALL and 2/Lt T.G. MORTIMER, all P.U.O.	
			Weather fine.	

W. M. Hore Lt Col
Commanding 25th Bn Liverpool Regt.

Army Form C. 2118.

WAR DIARY
and
INTELLIGENCE SUMMARY.
(*Erase heading not required.*)

Instructions regarding War Diaries and Intelligence Summaries are contained in F. S. Regs., Part II. and the Staff Manual respectively. Title pages will be prepared in manuscript.

Place	Date	Hour	Summary of Events and Information	Remarks and references to Appendices

9/5C 3

CONFIDENTIAL.

WAR DIARY

OF

25th Bn. KING'S LIVERPOOL REGIMENT.

From :- JULY 1st 1918.
To :- JULY 31st 1918.

(13)

WAR DIARY or INTELLIGENCE SUMMARY.

Army Form C. 2118.

25th Br. King's Liverpool Regt.

Place	Date	Hour	Summary of Events and Information	Remarks and references to Appendices
LAIRES	1-7-18		Weather fine – 3 Reinforcement officers arrived 2/Lt F.S. ROCKLEDGE, 2/Lt S.W.J.B. TUCKER & 2/Lt M.G. SINCLAIR and 7 ORs from Base.	App A
	2-7-18		Weather fine; Specimen of P.L.O. seen the whole of training as usual	App A
	3-7-18		Weather showery, training as usual	App A
	4-7-18		" " " "	App A
	5-7-18		" " " "	App A
	6-7-18		" " fine " "	App A
	7-7-18		" " " Bn marched to range and whole Bn put through three practices in non duty. 4 OR Reinforcement arrived from Base.	App A
	8-7-18		Weather thundery, training as usual – warning order to move to TANGRY AREA. Moving in at 6pm.	App A
	9-7-18		Weather showery, moved to HESTRUS	App A
HESTRUS	10-7-18		Weather fine, training as usual	App A
	11-7-18		" " " "	App A
	12-7-18		" " " "	App A

Army Form C. 2118.

WAR DIARY
INTELLIGENCE SUMMARY.
(Erase heading not required.)

25th Bn King's (Liverpool Regt)

Place	Date	Hour	Summary of Events and Information	Remarks and references to Appendices
HESTRUS	13.7.18		Battn inspected by General Sir H.S. HORNE, K.C.B., K.C.M.G. Weather fine	A.S.A
"	14.7.18		Church parade. Weather fine	A.S.A
"	15.7.18		Weather fine. Training as usual.	A.S.A
"	16.7.18		" " " "	A.S.A
"	17.7.18		" " " "	A.S.A
"	18.7.18		Weather showery. Thunder. Training as usual	A.S.A
"	19.7.18		" " " "	A.S.A
"	20.7.18		A & B Coys went to the line for instruction to 1st Division. Weather showery	A.S.A
"	21.7.18		Weather fine. Church parade. Div Cinema. Lt.Col C.E. Lembcke D.S.O. Northumberland Fus. arrived to take over the command of the Battn. Warning order to move to new area received 7.30pm	A.S.A
"	22.7.18		A & B Coys returned from line as per weather.	A.S.A
"	23.7.18		Battn moved by lorry to BRETENCOURT. Lt.Col W.M. HORE proceeded to 59th Div.	A.S.A
BERTRENCOURT	24.7.18		Reception Camp. Heavy rain & thunder. Inspection by Div. General, Major General Sir R.D. WHIGHAM, K.C.B., D.S.O.	A.S.A
	25.7.18		Prepared to move up to the trenches during the day	A.S.A

WAR DIARY
or
INTELLIGENCE SUMMARY.
(Erase heading not required.)

Army Form C. 2118.

2.8th Bn Kings (Liverpool)

Place	Date	Hour	Summary of Events and Information	Remarks and references to Appendices
	25/6/93	9 am	Bn. moved up to trenches. "B" Coy were shelled on the way, No.10825? Pt BRADBURY W. was the first Battn. casualty in all. From had 3.R. wounded. We relieved the 4.2nd Royal Highlanders of Canada. Relief was complete about 3.30am.	KiA KiA KiA KiA KiA KiA KiA KiA KiA KiA
	26/7/16	1.5 am 12 noon	A few gas shells came over, it was favourable got about 20 min. Casualty return Wounded 5. ORs (1st duty) The weather was very wet and uncomfortable. Patrols were sent out by A.B & C Coy's. Major J.M. TWEEDY 5th Northumberland Fusiliers joined the Bn. as 2nd in Command.	KiA KiA KiA KiA KiA KiA KiA KiA
	27/7/16	12 noon	Weather still raining. Little gubbing works. Casualty Return 2/Lt F.G. EVANS T/Coy 2/Lt F.P.COATES "C" Coy both wounded. Bomb No. 38189 S. Pte W. JOHNSTONE "C" Coy killed in action. Being the first man to be killed in action of "C" Coy.	KiA KiA KiA KiA
	28/7/16	12 Noon	Capt W.B. COCKBURN taken command of "C" Coy. Patrols went out Weather heavy. Trench very bad. Casualties nil.	

WAR DIARY or INTELLIGENCE SUMMARY

Army Form C. 2118.

25th Bn King's Liverpool Regt

Place	Date	Hour	Summary of Events and Information	Remarks and references to Appendices
	27/7/18		Patrol went out and met an enemy patrol in No man's land at approx S.12.a.45.80, but were not fit near them and fired on them with rifle fire. Enemy returned fire. As the first man in the train was on it, has been at present forward, to engage the enemy. If Royal Sussex Regt and we went back into Brigade Support. Weather fine.	
	29/7/18	3am	Casualty report. No 82878 Sgt F.W.H. SINGFIELD died of wounds. 1 O.R. wounded. Hon Lt & Q.M W.J.KEARY 2/6th SHERWOOD FORESTERS joined the batt. 2/Lt I.H.WALKER to hospital sick. Slight shelling during the day (10 gas shells)	
	30/7/18		Weather fine. Casualty report nil.	
	31/7/18	12 Noon	Weather fine. Quiet day.	
		9 p.m.	We relieved the 26th Bn R.W.F. Slight shelling during relief. Relief complete about 3am 1/8/18. Casualty report nil.	

Relieved
1.8.18

to E.Lembeke
Canal 25th Bn Prs Kings Shrop Regt

Army Form C. 2118.

WAR DIARY
or
INTELLIGENCE SUMMARY.
(Erase heading not required.)

ORIGINAL

CONFIDENTIAL

WAR DIARY

April 1st August 1917
To August 31st 1917

Place	Date	Hour	Summary of Events and Information	Remarks and references to Appendices

Instructions regarding War Diaries and Intelligence Summaries are contained in F. S. Regs., Part II. and the Staff Manual respectively. Title pages will be prepared in manuscript.

Army Form C. 2118.

WAR DIARY
or
INTELLIGENCE SUMMARY.
(Erase heading not required.)

2nd Bn King's Royal Rifles

Instructions regarding War Diaries and Intelligence Summaries are contained in F. S. Regs., Part II. and the Staff Manual respectively. Title pages will be prepared in manuscript.

Place	Date	Hour	Summary of Events and Information	Remarks and references to Appendices
MERCATEL SECTOR	1-8-18		Bn. Holding left front line Sector. Quiet day and casualties nil	AAA
	2-8-18		" " Casualties nil. Bruce	AAA
	3-8-18	1.30am	relieved by 15th Essex, 178th Bde. C+D Coys entrained at MARBLEARCH for BARLEY	AAA
		2.30a	Relief complete	AAA
		5-6am	A+B + HQ Coy entrained at BLAIRVILLE for BARLEY. Casualties 1 ORwounded. On arrival tps marched to BARLEY.	AAA
BARLEY	4-8-18		at BARLEY the Bn. Rested. Quiet day. Church Services & tps. Casualties nil	AAA
	5-8-16		Quiet day. Bn training	AAA
	6-8-18		Practice alarm. Lecture by all Officers & NCO's & Os & Gas Officer	AAA
		11-12noon	Demonstration by HAC. Demonstration Platoon	AAA
		5pm-6pm	Lecture by Brig-General T G COPE DSO Comdg. 176 Inf Bde in Lund warfare. Casualties nil	AAA
	7-8-18		Inspection of transport by Brig Gen COPE. Bn marched to see a tracer bullet demonstration by Lt Col Pluton	AAA
		5pm	Bn. Operat. Orders warning to move up line next day. Casualties nil	AAA
		6-7pm	Lecture by Divisional Commander. All Officers	AAA

WAR DIARY
or
INTELLIGENCE SUMMARY.
(Erase heading not required.)

Army Form C. 2118.

25th Bn "King's" Liverpool Regt

Place	Date	Hour	Summary of Events and Information	Remarks and references to Appendices
	8-8-18	1-0am	Bn operation orders No. 5 to move up line issued	AHA
		9.30am	Coys Commanders inspected the Bn. afterwards prepared to move.	
		5.50pm	Marched off	AHA
		7.0pm	Left BAVINCOURT.	
MERCATEL	9-8-18	12.30am	Arrived at MARBLE ARCH and relieved 15th ESSEX in support at CHAT MAIGRE. Casualties 1 OR wounded and 1 Horse killed	AHA, HA
SECTOR	10-8-18		Quiet day. 1 OR died of wounds.	HA
	11-8-18		Quiet day. A small not enemy [?] balloon messages dropped into our lines. A [?] Copy attached	HA
			It was sent at once to Bde HQ.	
	12-8-18		Quiet day. 1 OR accidentally injured	HA
	13-8-18		Quiet day. Casualties nil. Lt Col [?] made the defence scheme of CHAT MAIGRE.	HA
	14-8-18	4.30pm	Quiet day. Relieved 26th Bn RWF in front line. Visits in day light	HA
		11.30pm	Relief commenced. So late owing to RF Coy delaying relief. Casualties nil completed.	HA
	14-8-18		Secret Atty'd [?] When taking over orders were received that in case of enemy retirement we were to move forward and occupy enemy front line and at the [?] came the Colonel was visiting Bn orders are [?] from Bde to effect that special car was to be taken in case the enemy should use as a feast first raided	HA
			the Bde on my left	
	15-8-18		Patrol of RWF came in an reported enemy were still in occupation of their line	HA
			Quiet day. Casualties nil	

Army Form C. 2118.

WAR DIARY
or
INTELLIGENCE SUMMARY
(Erase heading not required.)

2/5th Bn King's (Liverpool Regt)

Place	Date	Hour	Summary of Events and Information	Remarks and references to Appendices
	16-8-18		Quiet day. Weather fine. Casualties nil. Two patrols went out under 2/Lt DICKENSON, STAGG and 2/Lt PHIPPS respectively, the first to reconnoitre MYRTLE SAP, the 2nd to reconnoitre route to rear of DOG S.A.P.	HQA
	17-8-18		Quiet day. Casualties nil. 3 patrols went out under 2/Lt ROBERTSON, WM. T.E. GEORGE + J A L BALLARD respectively, 1st to investigate our wire 2nd to MYRTLE SAP & 3rd to DOG SAP.	HQA
	18-8-18		Quiet day. Casualties 1 wounded. Two patrols went out 1st under 2/Lt DICKENSON + ROBERTSON as a fighting patrol, did not encounter the enemy, 2nd under 2/Lt STAGG & PHIPPS with the object of getting within 50yds of DOG SAP & listening for enemy movements.	HQA
	19-8-18		Quiet day. Casualties nil. Weather fine. Two patrols went out 1st under 2/Lt BALLARD + PHIPPS to reconnoitre 2 gun positions 2nd 2/Lt STAGG & GEORGE to reconnoitre a Bombing Post.	HQA
	20-8-18	4.30am	Quiet day. Bn relieved by 1/9th Bn R. SUSSEX. Relief commenced by each Coy moving to Coy Hd Qrs not able the relieving daylight, relief carried on at dusk.	HQA
		8pm	Orders received to send out 3 fighting patrols, these to get in touch with the enemy and establish an OBSERVATION LINE, & if there patrols fought in time a Coy was moved out of the line. The night patrol 2/Lt Wm ROBERTSON 1/OR middle patrol 2/Lt A L BALLARD & 1/OR left patrol 2/Lt A BLYTHE & 14 OR's, these patrols got in touch with enemy and established an observation line.	HQA

WAR DIARY
or
INTELLIGENCE SUMMARY.

(Erase heading not required.)

Army Form C. 2118.

25th Bn King's (Liverpool) Regt.

Place	Date	Hour	Summary of Events and Information	Remarks and references to Appendices
BRETENCOURT	20.8.18	11.30	Ruled canvas troops moved billets in BRETENCOURT	
	21.8.18	4.55am	The 3 Battns went out as reinforcements and took up positions through 176 Inf Bde.	
		12.35pm	Telegram from G.O.C. 59th Div. Congratulations on success of yesterday's operations informs C.O. and all concerned. Bn remains now to consolidate ground won and gain further touch with the enemy.	
		5pm	Orders received to take up Position in PURPLE LINE & as known tomorrow Aug 22nd. Orders issued.	
	22.8.18	1.30pm	Enemy aircraft very active all night, bombing in vicinity. Enemy aircraft came down in flames some distance away. Troops cleaning up.	
		12 Noon	Verbal orders received re plans to move BnHQ from BRETENCOURT to BRETENCOURT CHATEAU	
		3pm	Staff of 52nd Div. arrived. Colonel explained the ground in front of our line to 52nd Div. Intell. Officer.	
		3.30pm	Verbal Orders received on 'phone from 59th Div. Q. to move out Bn or out of billets into bivouacs. Ground reconnoitred and Bn moved at Beside in bivouacs. Remaining one Oiffr & 32nd Div. Bn HQ. in a hut.	
	23.8.18	4.50pm	Orders received to move Bn by march route to SAULTY. Orders were issued	
		6.15pm	Bn moved off.	
		10.30pm	Arrived billets SAULTY and bivouacs.	

Army Form C. 2118.

WAR DIARY
or
INTELLIGENCE SUMMARY.
(Erase heading not required.)

25th Bn King's (Liverpool)

Instructions regarding War Diaries and Intelligence Summaries are contained in F. S. Regs., Part II. and the Staff Manual respectively. Title pages will be prepared in manuscript.

Place	Date	Hour	Summary of Events and Information	Remarks and references to Appendices
SAULTY	24-8-18		Orders received to move to SAULTY LABRET and carry parties and standby	
"		4:30 pm	Arrived at SAULTY LABRET stand, entrained for BOUREC Q	
	25-8-18	4:30 am	Arrived at LILLERS and marched to BOURECQ.	
BOURECQ		6 am	Arrived BOURECQ Coy, spent in cleaning up.	
		11:30 am	Orders received to move to HAMET BILLETS. Orders received	
"	26-8-18	3 pm	Bn marched off by Coys and arrived which 16th R.SUSSEX Regt. 74th Div.	
		5:4pm	Bn arrived in new billets	
HAMET BILLETS	27-6-18		Quiet Day. Casualties nil. Bn Training	
	28-7-18		Quiet Day. Casualties " " to gala day, letter received from Ralph Ann and letter received from Bella, marked A and attached	
	29-7-18		Quiet day Casualties. Bn Training - Brig Gen. COPE spoke to the Bn on Parade, commenting on grith word done while in the MERCATEL sector. he also read us that the Divisional General had from the command another Division + received letter receiving from another General WHIGHAM K.C.B. D.S.O. on his leaving the Divisional another Div.	
	30-7-18		Quiet day Casualties nil Bn Training.	
	31-7-18		Quiet day Casualties nil Training as usual	
		4:15pm	Bn Orders received to move to St FLORIS. P.S. @ 10.6.0 at 6pm Bn detrained Bn marched off [?] at St FLORIS at 7-0pm and relieved 13th West Riding Regt.	

Army Form C. 2118.

WAR DIARY
or
INTELLIGENCE SUMMARY

(Erase heading not required.)

25th Bn King's Liverpool Regt.

Instructions regarding War Diaries and Intelligence Summaries are contained in F. S. Regs., Part II. and the Staff Manual respectively. Title pages will be prepared in manuscript.

Place	Date	Hour	Summary of Events and Information	Remarks and references to Appendices
ST FLORIS	31-8-18		West Riding Regt. This move forward was due to the Division having advanced	A/A

1st September 1918.

C. C. Embree
Lieut. Colonel
Commanding 25th Bn The King's Liverpool Regt T.F.

Army Form C. 2118.

WAR DIARY
or
INTELLIGENCE SUMMARY.
(Erase heading not required.)

Vol 5

CONFIDENTIAL.

WAR DIARY
of
25th BN. "THE KING'S" (LIVERPOOL REGIMENT)

From: 1st Sept. 1918.
To: 30th Sept. 1918.

4⁹

Confidential

Army Form C. 2118.

WAR DIARY
or
INTELLIGENCE SUMMARY

25th Bn "King's" Liverpool Regt.

(Erase heading not required.)

Instructions regarding War Diaries and Intelligence Summaries are contained in F.S. Regs., Part II. and the Staff Manual respectively. Title Pages will be prepared in manuscript.

Place	Date	Hour	Summary of Events and Information	Remarks and references to Appendices
ST FLORIS	1-9-18		Quiet Day. Weather fine. 120 ORs. Working Parties. Casualties NIL	
	2-9-18		Quiet Day. Weather fine. Companies training	
	3-9-18	10.30 am	176 Inf Bde Order No 125. received. Bde to relieve 174th Inf Bde in support.	
		11.30 am	B/Colbs went to LESTREM and relieve 15th Essex Regt. Bde Commanders came in and tires us that 2 Coys of the Unit which we were to relieve forward and under orders of G.O.C. 178th Inf Bde. Tactical Purposes and we were to move two of our Coys forward and relieve their two Coys.	
LESTREM		12. Noon	Bn moved off under 2nd in Command. Lt Colonel went to a senior officers Conference	
		3. pm	Bn arrived at LESTREM and relief completed of two rear Coys.	
		4 pm	A & B Coys moved forward to relieve the forward Coys. A Coy reported having relieved their HQ now at R.11 Central. Sheet 36a.	
		5.45 pm	B Coy relief complete. Position R.2.b.4.d. Sheet 36a. Weather fine. Casualties NIL. Bn. less two companies (Battle position) now held the line of the RIVER LAWE from R.9.a.10.80 thence along west bank of River to CANAL about L.34.d.20.90.	
	4-9-18		Weather fine.	
		11.15 am	Relieving up to this day the Bn would move forward and come under orders of G.O.C. 178 Inf. Bde for tactical purposes. Wire No BM 313 confirmed this.	
		2 pm	Bn. moved and Bn moved off and halted at about R.5.d.50.80. near (Pont Rochon) where 2nd in Command held a conference of officers and explained how he wanted the relief carried out.	
		3.30 pm	Bn. moved on to about M.2.c.90.40. near CARTER'S POST where Bn halted and	
		4.15 pm		

WAR DIARY
or
INTELLIGENCE SUMMARY

Army Form C. 2118.

25th Bn "King's" Liverpool Regt

Place	Date	Hour	Summary of Events and Information	Remarks and references to Appendices
	4.9.18		Found Bn HQ of the Bn which we had to relieve the West Riding Regt. A & B Coys had been under the orders of their C.O. A Coy supports to their right flank and B Coy support to their left flank. There the Coys then had orders to push up and to through the West Riding with "C" in support of right and "D" Coy in support of left flank. The post line Coys were to rest on the RUE DU BACQUEROL whilst support Coys about 250-300 yds in rear. The West Ridings were thought to be about 30 yds in rear of the flank - attainment objective vc90 to the RUE TILLELOY. Northern boundary being gulli line running E and W at R.3.a. 40.99 and southern boundary being line running E to W at A.7.d. 05.00.	13/7
		6.30 pm	C & D Coys arrived.	
		9.30 pm	Bn HQ assembled at about M.10.c. 40.90. Fd in HAILEBURY RD.	
			The A & B Coys with C & D Coys in support reached RUE DU BACQUERO-	
			-LAY and the West Ridings moved back. They reports complete absence of enemy.	
			A/- Bn moved forward in dawn with the object of reaching RUE	
	5.9.18		TILLELOY	
			Bn HQ arrived to HARLECH CASTLE about M.10.a. 50.12. Orders received from B.C.B. that he had made dispositions at TWO TREE Fm N2 c.1070 and were held up. He was ordered to try and push round N. side & try punch the enemy out.	
		9 am	A Coy R.F. and Coy report having reached their objective and are pushing a trench APPROBANT N 13.b. 20.80 to N 8.a. 50.30 with enemy holding a trench about	

Army Form C. 2118.

WAR DIARY
or
INTELLIGENCE SUMMARY   2 5th Bn Kings own Liverpool Regt

(Erase heading not required.)

Place	Date	Hour	Summary of Events and Information	Remarks and references to Appendices
250 yds in front	5-9-18		A Coy's barrage repeated & B Coy got information B Coy could not move round TWO TREE F.M. on the N. side, tried to	#29 #29
		12 noon	move forward thy' northern side and get in touch with A Coy. they met with heavy hostile M.G. fire and sustained heavy casualties. Nº 1 & Nº 3 Blob as platoons kept in position on left as strong point until 1 Platoon of left support Coy attempted to push forward SOUTH of TWO TREE FM. afterwards but was held up by heavy M.G. fire from TWO TREE FM and N7.b.60.60 our position was 3 platoons holding WINDY POST, one platoon at N.1.b.50.05 and one platoon at N.1.d.30.70. two platoons in PICCADILLY at about N7.b.10.90 our movement by day impossible in N.1.d. area. Estimating enemy at TWO TREE FM. 4 M.G.s & 1 TM. and 20 rifles and 50 rifles. LOW casualties in these two Coy's. Lewis officer + 30 ORs and the remaining platoon of left support Coy's 1 in reserve at Bn H.Q. and one moving up platoon from WINDY Post to N.1.a central area stand as but for artillery fire on TWO TREE FM and S.E.	#29 #29 #29 #29
			The remainder of the day was spent in consolidating. Casualties. 2/Lt. J.A CLAYTON, 2/Lt- S.M. J.B. TUCKER 2/Lt A. DIRKIN wounded. 8 other ranks killed, one OR. missing believed killed, and 30 other ranks wounded.	

Army Form C. 2118.

WAR DIARY
or
INTELLIGENCE SUMMARY
(Erase heading not required.)

25th Bn "D" King Liverpool Regt

Place	Date	Hour	Summary of Events and Information	Remarks and references to Appendices
	6.9.18	6 pm	Day spent in consolidating. Relief arriving from unit to take salient. Casualties nil.	HW
	7.9.18		Quiet Day. Broken for Bn relief. 1 O.R. wounded 5/9/18 died of wounds in C.C.S.	HW
Pont du Hem.		1.35 pm	Relief complete and Bn moved back to "bullets" at Pont du Hem. Casualties 1 O.R. wounded outpost.	HW
	8.9.18		Quiet day. Bn was in Bde Support. Position to be held (M.22.c.30.00. to Esquin Post about M.11.c.50.30.) Wire reconnoitred. Casualties nil. 1 O.R. died of wounds at grex up to wounded 5/9/18	HW
"	9.9.18		Quiet day. men reading & bathing B. Coy. were shelled during night of g.m. Casualties 3 ORs wounded.	HW
"	10.9.18		Quiet day. Weather showery. Casualties nil. 1 O.R. reported wounded on 5/9/18 died of wounds in CCS	HW
"	11.9.18		Quiet day. Casualties nil weather showery.	HW
	12.9.18		Quiet day. Casualties nil.	HW
	13.9.18	9.10 am 1.30 pm	Orders received for Bde relief. We were relieved by 1st Bn Essex Regt & taken for Bn relief. Moved back to Div. Movn Bn HQ at L.36.97.5 point Wise Keld from M.3.C.30.50 to G.33.a.50.50. Casualties nil. 2 Lt S.W.R. Tucker reported wounded 5/9/18 died of wounds in C.C.S.	HW HW

2449 Wt. W14957/Mg0 750,000 1/16 J.B.C. & A. Forms/C.2118/12.

WAR DIARY
INTELLIGENCE SUMMARY

Army Form C. 2118.

25th Bn Kings (Liverpool) Regt

Place	Date	Hour	Summary of Events and Information	Remarks and references to Appendices
LA GORGUE	14.9.18		Quiet day. Weather fine. Casualties Nil.	Nil
	15.9.18		" " " "	AEA
			2 wounded in C.C.S previously reported wounded 5/9/18	
			Bn training.	
	16.9.18		Weather fine. C. Coy shelled at intervals during the day. Casualties	AEA
			Nil. 1 OR died of wounds. reported wounded 5/9/18	
	17.9.18		Quiet day. Bn training. Weather fine. Casualties nil.	Nil
	18.9.18		Quiet day. Bn training. Rear parties A B C bullets & medical school.	Nil
			Weather fine. Casualties Nil.	Nil
	19.9.18		Weather fine. A Coy relieved. Two cases of men shelter.	Nil
	20.9.18		Weather fine. Bn training. Coys training. Divisional mass prayer. Enemy C Coy shelling—enemy 11am.	Nil
			1 OR slightly wounded. 13 HEs shelling near 9.30 PM & 11.30 PM	N.2.0.h
	21.9.18		1 temporarily evacuated position.	
			Weather fine. C Coy shelled. Several rounds of new position fly. Rty in rear of battery 7-8 PM Bn training	
			2 OR prisoners on 19/9/18 (Privates & Anker by Army Council many Fields pres on a Coy speakers	
			Aft 4 OR awarded MM for gallantry report WDA in sector 5-10 & 9.18 (Two Trees Farm)	R.A.C.h.n
	22.9.18		Weather showery. Church Parade. Day spent in rest. Casualties Nil.	A.A.h
	23.9.18		B Awd men E & 36 C 15.25. B Coy man killed E & 36 C 75. Enemy pinto B + C were	P.M.N.i7

Army Form C. 2118.

WAR DIARY or INTELLIGENCE SUMMARY
(Erase heading not required.)

25th Bn The King's (Liverpool Regt)

Place	Date	Hour	Summary of Events and Information	Remarks and references to Appendices
LA GORGUE	23/9/18		Troops to I.O. lecture to Scouts w/B.H.Q. Slight shelling during night. Weather fine	10th C.Lr
	24/9/18		Weather fine. Working parties on wire & filter clearing near Bn HQ. Casualties Nil	Rim C.Lr
	25/9/18		Weather showery. Working parties on previous day. Casualties Nil	P.m C.Lr
	26/9/18		Weather fine. Working parties as before. Casualties Nil.	10m C.Lr
	27/9/18		Showery. Training. Working party in afternoon of pellets 2367 5 Casualties Nil	Rth C.Lr
	28/9/18		Showery. Bn Training in AM. Attack coys bathing. Casualties Nil	10w C.Lr
	29/9/18		Bathing. Bn received orders at 4.30 PM to relieve 26th Bn RWF at HARLECH CASTLE. Orders issued to coys. Relief begun	10m C.Lr
HARLECH CASTLE	30/9/18		Relief completed 1.15 AM. 4 AM Two Portuguese prisoners of war sent to B.H.Q. by C.C. by sentry to war escort from LILLE. They were questioned returned & sent to Bde H.Q. at 9 AM. 2 Patrols of C by reconnitred Trenches & ground between WINDY POST & THE TREE FARM & got into touch with enemy in PICCADILLY TRENCH. Casualties Nil. Weather showery.	10m C.Lr

C. E. Lembeler
LIEUT. COL.
Commanding 25th Bn The King's (Liverpool Regt.)

Army Form C. 2118.

WAR DIARY
or
INTELLIGENCE SUMMARY.   25th B/n The Kings (Liverpool Regt)
(Erase heading not required.)

Place	Date	Hour	Summary of Events and Information	Remarks and references to Appendices
			ADDENDUM:—	
	5.9.18		Names of N.C.O's & MEN who were awarded the Military Medal— are as follows:—	
			407114. Sergt. WRAGG. F.	
			108037. Sergt. WOOD W.	
			108386. Pte. COOPER. G.W.	Mem
			82751. Pte. GILMOUR. E.H.	

Confidential

Original War Diary
of
25th Bn. The King's (Liverpool Regiment)

From: 1st Octr, 1918
To: 31st Octr, 1918.

Army Form C. 2118.

WAR DIARY
INTELLIGENCE SUMMARY.
(Erase heading not required.)

25th Bn The Kings (Liverpool Regiment)

Place	Date	Hour	Summary of Events and Information	Remarks and references to Appendices
HARLECH CASTLE	1.10.18	04.30	Gas successfully projected by R.E. on enemy's position PICCADILLY TRENCH & TWO TREE FARM from our G & D Coys. Position considerable enemy shelling between 1900 & 2100. Casualties one officer 2/Lt Omerod wounded. M & Lts Murray McKellen	M & Mc
	2.10.18	0730	Attack on TWO TREE FARM on a two company frontage supported by Artillery M.G.s	
		0815	C Coy (on right) reported 1st & 2nd objectives taken	
		0820	A & B Coys (centre & left) took their objective TWO TREE FARM & Trench N of left	
		1000	Companies consolidating. Patrols pushed out.	
		1115	Attack Bn advanced 1200 Bn in touch with Bn of Bn Pott on left	
		1515	Bn dropped on Minus — Formed if RUE PETILLON left flank on ETAM HALL N35-00.35 Right flank BROMPTON ROAD N3C6505. Two Coys in outpost line + one in Support. Bn H Q N2C85.20 Patrols in close intercourse on right & left. All objectives gained. Prisoners taken 9.3 Light M.G.s 7 Heavy M.G. Casualties 2/Lt Foxall wounded, 47 O.R. killed, Capt Gorman 2/Lts Brownbury, Bean, Blythe & Jervis wounded 2/Lt Jackson wounded slightly. 34 O.R. wounded. Bn was relieved by the 19th London Regt and 6th Bn Bruce Artillery at HARLECHCASTLE	Battle

Army Form C. 2118.

WAR DIARY
INTELLIGENCE SUMMARY.
(Erase heading not required.)

2nd BN "The Kings" (Liverpool Regiment)

Place	Date	Hour	Summary of Events and Information	Remarks and references to Appendices
				Map Ref: Sheet 36NW4 1/10,000
HARLECH CASTLE	3-10-16	0015	Relief completed	
			Bn. moved to AU NOUVEAU MONDE. Other ranks proceeded Bn. proceeded by 'bus	
			Two O.R. returned 2/10/16 sick & wounded Australian C.C.S.	R.M.Chr
AU NOUVEAU MONDE	4/10/28		Bn moved by bus at 1700 to ERQUINGHEM SWITCH rear line. 1 O.R. wounded 2-10-17	
MONDE			and joining Australian C.C.S.	O.R.Chr
ERQUINGHEM	5-10-16		Weather fine. Slight enemy shelling in morning. O. Retained Court Martial at dinner	
SWITCH			1 O.R. returned 2-10-18 sick & wounded. of March 9 Australian C.C.S.	R.M.Chr
	6-10-16		Weather fine. Orders received to move to MAURITS front + VERSES Post system covered	
			By pieces 46 by 2nd & Corps Left up post A & B Coys front portion (Mabcdef I23 & w)	
			Bn. H.Q.S. as I201 b9.55 - D Coy in support I21 c902ZZ - E Coy in Reserve	
			in left sector SWITCH I13R & I132. On Outer enemy shelling in Forest	
			June supported near 178 Bde H.a. Shortly after Bean Coys to Humes" Casualties RMChr	
				1 O.R. wounded	
LA VESSE	7/10/16	0105	Coys in position. Weather fine. Casualties 2 O/R wounded	R.M.
SWITCH	8-10-16		Fort Garrack taken ? I232 36.30. I23 340.40. I/2 co. to send H.T. Report	R.L.
			Weather showery. 10.R. reported wounded 5-9-16 died of wounds	
	9-10-16		Weather wet. B Coy shelled at night. Post at I23A touts raided by enemy & captured. 2/LT J.B. CARSON & 11 OR.missing	
			believed POW. V.2/Lt GEORGE & 5 OR. who accompanied 2/Lt PAGET-WILKES R.F.A. on a patrol were engaged by	L.P.
			enemy & captured, believed POW.	

WAR DIARY
or
INTELLIGENCE SUMMARY

Army Form C. 2118.

25th Bn. The Kings (Liverpool Regt.)

Place	Date	Hour	Summary of Events and Information	Remarks and references to Appendices
LA VESSEE SECTOR	10-10-18		Weather wet. Casualties nil. 1 O.R. killed in action. 1 O.R. wounded who was previously reported missing on 8th. He was found by a reconnoitring patrol and 2/Lt TE GEORGE and 5 O.R. reported missing returned.	
			2/Lts E.L. PATERSON, H.T. WOODS, J.H. WISHIER, E. LANE, S.H. LEES, K. GIBSON G.E. BRIGGS & W.B. JAMES joined the Bn.	
	11-10-18		Weather fine. Casualties nil. Inter Coy relief - A & B went into front line C in support & D in reserve.	
	12-10-18		Weather changeable. Casualties nil. Bn HQ moved to DAISY POST. T 15 c 8 5 75.	
	13-10-18		Weather fine. Casualties nil. Two patrols went out to reconnoitre enemy's line back, & neither touch with enemy & came back.	
	14-10-18		Weather fine. Casualties nil. B Coy on night went forward, Bn was ready to advance to their line when news came that the Bn on the right had been counter attacked and had come back to their original line. Bn stood fast. Two patrols went out under 2Lt WOODS & LANE to Recce village of WEZ MACQUART but the clean sweep the patrols returned reporting village clear but they had been fired on by M.G.s from wood on the right.	

Army Form C. 2118.

WAR DIARY
or
INTELLIGENCE SUMMARY. 25th Bn The King's (Leool Regt.)

(Erase heading not required.)

Instructions regarding War Diaries and Intelligence
Summaries are contained in F. S. Regs., Part II.
and the Staff Manual respectively. Title pages
will be prepared in manuscript.

Place	Date	Hour	Summary of Events and Information	Remarks and references to Appendices
LAVESSEE SECTOR	15.10.18		Weather fine. Casualties nil. Two patrols one under Lt CARTER, went out to ascertain if F^ms L'ER PERONNERIE and LA BLEUE were garrisoned by the enemy, the first named farm was held and the second were no traces of the enemy were found.	AM
		15.00	Bn advanced and occupied the line F^m L'EPERONNERIE — F^m LA BLEUE	AM
		22.30	Bn relieved by 14th ROYAL SUSSEX relief completed Bn marched back	AM
ERQUINGHEM	16.10.18		to bivouacs at ERQUINGHEM SWITCH. Bayonet training. Deaths with Casualties NIL	AM
	17.10.18	01.00	Orders received to move up to DAISY POST AREA in Square I 16. 9.10	AM
		07.20	Bn moved off	AM
DAISY POST		12.00	" arrived in new area. Weather fine. Casualties. Orders received to move forward.	AM
	18.10.18	8.00	Bn moved off	AM
ST ANDRE		12.30	" arrived at ST ANDRE and received orders to move forward if possible.	AM
			C.O. made a speech to the Bn	AM
		14.00	Bn moved off found bridges at MARQUETTE blown up. Bn went over the river to Pearl bridge. Marched through MADELEINE (Suburb of LILLE)	AM
			Here the Bn advance received the Bn with rejoicing, &	AM

T2134. Wt. W708—776. 500000. 4/15. Sir J.C. & S.

WAR DIARY
INTELLIGENCE SUMMARY — 25th Bn King's (Liverpool) Regt

Army Form C. 2118.

Place	Date	Hour	Summary of Events and Information	Remarks and references to Appendices
MADELEINE	18-10-18		Old men + women crying and dancing with joy.	H.E.H
		16.00	Arrived WASQUEHAL. A & D Coys were outpost Coys with C & B in support. Weather fine. Casualties nil.	H.E.H H.E.H H.E.H
	19-10-18	07.30	Bn moved forward in accordance with orders received. Bn advanced through 96 R.W.F who were at HEM. Reached 1st objective.	H.E.H H.E.H
		14.00	Bn advanced and reached 2nd objective (Line NORTH & SOUTH through TEMPLEUVE - NECHIN) about 16.00. Bn H.T.R at F.M. DE SAUL. Weather fine. Bn had marched 30 miles and gone into action in 36 hours still. Casualties nil.	H.E.H H.E.H H.E.H
	20-10-18		Weather fine. Casualties nil.	H.E.H
		11.00	Reached first objective. (Line of TOURNAI — ROUBAIX railway)	H.E.H
			B.Coy moved forward to line of ESCAULT River bank.	H.E.H
		16.00	received objective, D Coy moved up in support with A & C Coys in reserve at LE CROUZET. Bn H.Q. at SAUFRIEU F.M. Enemy shelled during the night with gas shell. H.Q moved	H.E.H H.E.H H.E.H
	21-10-18		Weather fine. Casualties Lt J.M PATERSON + 1 O.R wounded. B. Coy commenced to bridge the River ESCAULT the R.E. later turned up and built a pontoon bridge which he used as a ferry boat.	H.E.H H.E.H H.E.H

Army Form C. 2118.

WAR DIARY
or
INTELLIGENCE SUMMARY. 25th Bn King's (Liverpool Regt)

(Erase heading not required.)

Instructions regarding War Diaries and Intelligence Summaries are contained in F.S. Regs., Part II. and the Staff Manual respectively. Title pages will be prepared in manuscript.

Place	Date	Hour	Summary of Events and Information	Remarks and references to Appendices
	21-10-18	16:00	"B" Coy crossed the ESCAUT but could not get objects as they were over their waists in water in the marsh. Posts were established on the bridge between Road Relch.	A/a
			Weather fine. Casualties 1 OR Killed, Lt E.L. PATERSON and 22 OR wounded.	A/a
	22.10.18		Orders for relief by 9/6 D.L.I. received. Congratulatory messages from Bde. (if attached)	A/a
		20:00	Relief complete. Arrived at TOUFFLERS at 22:00 Bn all in by 22:35	A/a
TOUFFLERS	23.10.18		Weather fine. Casualties 3 OR wounded.	A/a
			Day spent in cleaning up.	A/a
	24-10-18		Weather fine. Casualties nil.	A/a
			Bn Training	A/a
	25.10.18		Weather fine. Casualties nil. Lt E.L. PATERSON reported wounded 22-10-18 Died of wounds. Congratulatory message from XI Corps (is attached)	A/a
	26-10-18		Weather fine. Casualties nil	A/a
			Training	A/a
	27.10.18		Weather fine. Casualties nil. Church Parade. No training	A/a
	28-10-18		Weather fine. Casualties nil. Bn Training	A/a
			Awarded Military Medal. Date of Award 26/10/18	A/a

No 108 487 Pte F. TICKLE No 25232 Pte J. KIRKHAM No 407/23 Pte F. WALTERS & No 82719 Pte L. RECKOVER

Army Form C. 2118.

WAR DIARY
or
INTELLIGENCE SUMMARY.
(Erase heading not required.)

Instructions regarding War Diaries and Intelligence Summaries are contained in F. S. Regs., Part II. and the Staff Manual respectively. Title pages will be prepared in manuscript.

Place	Date	Hour	Summary of Events and Information	Remarks and references to Appendices
TOUFFLERS	29-10-18		Weather fine. Casualties nil. Bn training.	AEK
	30-10-18		Weather fine. Casualties nil. Bn training. Congratulatory message received from Army Commander on recent advance.	AEK
	31-10-18		Weather fine. Casualties nil. Bn training. Presentation parade to give medal ribbon to 108487 PTE F. TICKLE, 25232 PTE J. KIRKHAM, 407123 PTE F. WALTERS, and Nº 82757 PTE E. H. GILMOUR all four men having been awarded the Military Medal for gallantry in action.	AEK

C. E. Knuckle
LIEUT. COL. COMMDG.
25th. Bn. "THE KING'S" (LIVERPOOL REGT.)

GA490/14.

H.Q., FIFTH ARMY,
GENERAL STAFF.
(O)

Report on operations carried out
by the 25th Bn. King's Liverpool Regt.
Oct 18th — 21st 1918.

22

General Staff Circular No. 13.

Amendment No. 1. in file 41.

General Headquarters
D. A. G.
3rd Echelon

Will you please have
enclosed attached to October
War Diary — Omission greatly
regretted [signature] 5/11

AND ADJT:
25th. Bn. "THE KING'S" (LIVERPOOL REGT.)

5-XI-18

25th Bn."The King's" L'pool Regt.)

565/19/I
29.10.18

    The Brigade Commander has much pleasure in forwarding the attached correspondence for information and communication to all ranks of your Battalion.

29..10..18
          (sd.) G.E.Mansergh;
          Capt. A/Brigade Major.
          176th Infantry Brigade.

176th Inf.Bde.

G.S.
27.10.18.

    The Divisional Commander is very pleased to have received the attached correspondence which is forwarded for transmission to the 25th Battn. King's Liverpool Regt.

          (sd.) R.S.Follett.

27th October 1918.
          Lieut.Colonel.
          G.S. 59th Division.

59th Division.
          XI Corps G.S. 67/37

    The Corps Commander has much pleasure in forwarding the attached message of appreciation from the Army Commander.

          (sd.) J.Brind.

XI Corps.
26.10.18.
          B.G., G.S.

XI Corps. (2)
          Fifth Army;
          G.A.490/14.
          25th Oct.1918.

    I am to request you to convey to the 25th Bn.King's Liverpool Regt. the Army Commander's appreciation of the dash and determination shewn by that Battalion during its advance on October 18th., 19th., 20th. and 21st, and his appreciation also of its endurance and gallantry which reflect great credit on all ranks.

          (sd.) C.B.B.White.
          Major-General, G.S.

59th Division.   G.S. 67/36.

    The Corps Commander has much pleasure in forwarding the Army Commander's remarks on the patrol carried out by 2/Lieut. SAYER, 25th Bn. King's Liverpool Regiment.

                                        (sd.) J. Brind,

XI Corps.
27/10/18.   B.G., G.S.

<u>XI Corps.</u>   Fifth Army.
                                                      G.A.506/2.
                                                        24th Oct.1918.

    I am to thank you for the reports forwarded under your G.S. 67/36 of the 23rd instant and to request you to convey to those concerned the Army Commander's appreciation, not only of the information contained in the reports, but also of the excellent manner in which they were drawn up.

                                                       (sd.) C.B.B.White,
                                                           Major-General, G.S.

2/5th K. Liverpool Regt.
2/6th R. Welch Fus.
2/4th R. Sussex Regt.
176th L.T.M. Bty.

Ref 176th Inf Bde Order No. 138

On completion of relief Battalions will be billeted in TOUFFLERS area (S.23)

Billeting Officers & NCO's have been obtained from Battn. Transport lines. They will meet units at fork roads G.24.c. 70.00 and conduct them to their billets.

J P Brinley
Captain & Brigade Major
176th Infantry Brigade

22/10/18

I.15.d.5.3. aaa PALI will form a strong defensive flank to the left as far as the river aaa A/QENO will detail one section of M.G. from Reserve for this purpose (one section A/QENO will continue to be attached to forward Bns & the remaining sections will be in Brigade Reserve) aaa From this line strong patrols will move forward and establish posts as follows aaa ROMI about I.28.a.3.3. and I.22.c.2.6. aaa PALI about I.22.b.4.2 - I.16.d.3.0. and I.16.c.5.3 aaa Left hand post of JUGU will be I.28.d.0.3. aaa The capture of the high ground in J.19 and J.25 will be carried out by 176 and 178 Inf. Bdes. in accordance with the following instructions aaa Brigades will advance simultaneously from the line of the road O.4.central to HAVRON - OBIGIES aaa General line of advance will be approximately along the right (Rt. Divl Boundary O.1 cent. to O.6 cent) and left Divisional Boundaries respectively aaa As these two Brigades advance the detachments will turn inwards and press up the southern spur to MONT ST. AUBERT I.28.29 & 30 and north spurs of MONT de la TRINITE I.23 & I.24 respectively aaa To perform this operation posts will be established by ROMI on the low ground to sweep the reentrances to cover movement of these detachments on the high ground aaa PALI will advance along the Northern Boundary aaa The actual time for this operation will be notified later aaa. DAMA will be prepared

Secret

76 Inf Bde Order No 138   Copy No 6

Ref. Sheet 37 1/40000   22/10/16

1. The 71 Inf Bde will be relieved by 177 Inf Bde
in the line now held on 22/23rd Oct 1916 as follows:-
   20th R. Fusiliers will be relieved by 2/6 D of L
   17th Sussex   "   "   S. L. R.
   8th R W F   "   " 15 Essex
   11th Cheshire   "   " 17 Welsh

2. Guides at the rate of one platoon per
company and 1 per Bn H.Q. will be detailed
as follows:-
   OC 17 Sussex will arrange for guides to
be at River House H.23.c.7.8 at 1500
   OC 20 R Fusiliers will arrange for guides to
be at Bn HQ H.22.a.3.95 at 1500
   An advance party will be attached
to OC 15 Essex Regt to take over billets
vacated by 76 R W Fus.
   Great care should be taken in the
selection of guides.

3. During the hours of daylight, sections
will march in file along the side of
the road at 50 yards interval. After
dark companies will march in file

4. All other details of relief will be
arranged direct between COs concerned

5. Destination of Bns on relief will be
notified later

PALI.
DAMA.
ROMI.

S.843/I
22.10.18

Reference 176th Inf Bde. Warning Order No 137.

Battns. of the 176th Inf Bde will be relieved by Battns. of the 177th Inf Bde. as follows :-

25th KRR pools will be relieved by   2/6th Durham L.I.
27th R.Sussex   "   "   "   "   11th Somerset L.I.
26th R.W. Fus   "   "   "   "   15th Essex Regt.

Acknowledge

22/10/18.

J. Mann-----
Captain & Brigade Major
176 Infantry Brigade.

Divisional Commander.

Copy of Congratulatory letter from ~~Brigadier~General.~~ received from 176th INFANTRY BRIGADE.

" With reference to the request of the Divisional Commander, herewith report on operations carried out by the 25th Bn. "The King's" (Liverpool Regt.)

The 25th Bn. "The King's" (Liverpool Regt.) marched from Farm du Biez, CHAPELLE D'Armentieres at dawn on Oct 18th and reached ST ANDRE at 1.0. p.m. where the O.C. Battalion gave them a short address.

The Bn. then continued to march to WASQUEHAL, reaching there at 6.0. p.m.

At dawn on Oct. 19th the Bn. continued to march to HEM and passed through the 26th Bn. The Royal Welch Fussrs, and became part of the advanced guard to the Brigade.

It reached HULANS at 3.0 p.m. advancing in Artillery formation across country, thus the Bn. covered 30 miles in 36 hours.

On Oct. 20th the Bn. continued the advance and reached the Western bank of L'ESCAULT.

On Oct 21st by 5.0 p.m. 1½ Coys had crossed by pontoon to the EASTERN bank of the river in face of enemy resistance from M.gs. T.Ms & Snipers. "

(Sd.) T. G. COPE.
Brig. Genl.
commdg. 176th INFANTRY BRIGADE.

21.10.18.

(2)

6. The command will pass from G.O.C. 176 Inf Bde to G.O.C. 177 Inf Bde on completion of relief.

7. Completion of relief to be reported immediately by wire to these HQrs by

8. 176 Inf Bde Report Centre will close at I 25 a 80.35 at 1700 and at same hour 176 Inf Bde HQrs will close at H 26 b 00.50 reopening at TOUFFLERS G 2) at the same hour.

9. Acknowledge.

F B Mere-lly
Captain a Bde Major
176 Inf Bde.

Distribution :-
Copies 1 + 2   59th Div.
       3   177 Inf Bde
       4   193"
       5   170"
       6   25 K L Regt.
       7   26 R W Fus.
       8   17 R Surrey Regt.
       9   176 L Arty
     10   199 & 200 M G C
     11   296 Coy R E
     12   G.O.C.
     13   B.M.
     14   S.C.   16 } War Diary
     15   S.O.   17 }

XI Corps G.S. 67/37.

59th Division.

The Corps Commander has much pleasure in forwarding the attached message of appreciation from the Army Commander.

XI Corps.
26/10/18.

B.G.,G.S.

General Headquarters
A. A. G.
3rd Echelon

Herewith attached papers & documents. Will you please pin these to October War Diary already sent.

Regretting omission.

4.XI.18   N Stagg 2/Lt AND ADJT.
25h. Bn. "THE KING'S" (LIVERPOOL REGT.)

Fifth Army,
G.A. 400/14.
25th Oct., 1918.

XI Corps. (2).

    I am to request you to convey to the 25th Bn King's Liverpool Regt. the Army Commander's appreciation of the dash and determination shown by that Battalion during its advance on October 18th., 19th., 20th, and 21st., and his appreciation of its endurance and gallantry which reflect great credit on all ranks.

Major-General, G.S.

to move at ½ hour's notice from 10.00. aaa
Advanced Brigade HQrs will move to I.25.a.2.4
on first objective being gained. aaa All messages
will be delivered here after 10.00. aaa
Subsequent moves will be notified later. aaa
ACKNOWLEDGE.

JUZI.
0520.

L Murphy
Captain & Brigade Major

"A" Form.
MESSAGES AND SIGNALS.

Army Form C.2121
(in pads of 100.)
No. of Message _____

Prefix	Code	m.	Words	Charge	This message is on a/c of:	Recd. at ____ m.
			Sent			Date
Office of Origin and Service Instructions.			At ____ m.		_____ Service.	From
			To			
			By		(Signature of "Franking Officer.")	By

TO
ROMI.	BQENO.	Corps Mounted Troops.
DAMA.	KAQO.	DADA.	JUGI.	Signal officer
PALI.	MOHA.	JUGV.	JUVA.	Lt Taylor 470 Bbry
				Staff Captain

| Sender's Number | Day of Month. | In reply to Number. | AAA |
| * RM349. | 18th. | | |

Inf. concerning enemy is given in RM 350 to all concerned aaa The advance will be resumed at 0930 Oct 18th aaa XI Corps Mounted Troops will move so as to be in position by 0930 establishing posts L.25.c.50.30. – L.19.a.10.00. – K.18. central aaa Bridges to be completed by midnight are at K.20.d.50.10. and K.20.d. 70.10. also at K.21.a.30.80. – K.15.a.80.10. – MARQUETTE – K.9.b.40.20. aaa Corps cavalry will ascertain if enemy are holding line R.9. R.10. L.27. L.20. L.13. L.14. – the canal L.1.c & d. and if clear to push on. aaa Task of JU21 will be to secure inner line of LILLE defences East of City general line FLERS – L.32.a. – L.20.a. aaa Rt flank of Boe directed on L.20.d.0.0. left flank on L.8.c.0.0. boundary between Battalions main road L.14.c.65.40. –

L.15.d.20.10.

From				
Place				
Time				

The above may be forwarded as now corrected. (Z)

Censor.   Signature of Addressor or person authorised to telegraph in his name.

* This line should be erased if not required.

"A" Form,
MESSAGES AND SIGNALS.

Army Form C.2121 (in pads of 100.)

Sender's Number.	Day of Month.	In reply to Number.	AAA
* B.M.349	18		

aaa on reaching above line outpost observation line will be pushed forward aaa Bde. H.Q. will close Fme. de GIBET. K.7.c. 20.30. at 1030 and open K.24.c.50.80. at same hour aaa B/QENO and KAQO. will act in accordance with B.A.148 of 16th aaa added DAMA ROMI B/QENO. KAQO. MOHA. who will acknowledge repeated all concerned.

From JUZI.
Place
Time 0130.

XI CORPS GENERAL STAFF.

Report on Operations K.L.R

Subject.
No. 67/37   Date. 23/10   Time. 1150

	Initials.	Time.	Action.
G.O.C.			
A.D.C.			
B.G., G.S.			
G.S.O.2.(O)			
G.S.O.2.(T)			
G.S.O.2.(I)			
G.S.O.3.			
C.M.G.O.			
A.Q.			
Q.			
A.			
G.O.C.R.A.			
O.E.			
A.D.Sigs.			
D.D.M.S.			
A.P.M.			
Chem. Advr.			

Please pass quickly in above order.

XI Corps G.S.67/37.

Fifth Army.

Forwarded.

I think the Army Commander would be interested to read this report of the energy and determination shown during the recent advance by the 25th Bn. King's Liverpool Regt.

XI Corps.
23/10/18.

Lieut. General,
Commanding XI Corps.

XI Corps G.S.67/37.
59th Div. G.871.

XI Corps.

I give an account below of the operations carried out by the 25th Bn. King's Liverpool Rgt.

The 25th Bn. King's Liverpool Regt. marched from FM du BIEZ, CHAPELLE d'ARMENTIERES at dawn on October 18th and reached ST. ANDRE at 1.0 p.m. The Battalion continued the march to WASQUEHAL reaching there at 6.0 p.m.

At dawn on October 19th the march was continued to HEM, where the Battalion passed through the 26th Bn. Royal Welch Fusiliers, and became part of the Advanced Guard. It reached HULANS at 3.0 p.m., advancing in artillery formation across country, covering a total distance of 30 miles in 33 hours.

On October 20th the Battalion continued the advance and reached West Bank of L'ESCAUT.

On October 21st by 5.0 p.m. $1\frac{1}{2}$ Companies had crossed the river by pontoon in face of enemy resistance from Machine Guns and Trench Mortars.

22/10/18.

(sd) W.M.Smyth, Major Gen.
Commanding 59th Division.

"A" Form,
MESSAGES AND SIGNALS.

Army Form C.2121
(in pads of 100.)
No. of Message_____

Prefix____ Code____ m.	Words	Charge	This message is on a/c of:	Recd. at____ m.
	Sent			Date____
Office of Origin and Service Instructions.	At____ m.		____Service.	From____
	To			By____
	By		(Signature of "Franking Officer.")	

TO Rom: B/O CHO   bapt old troops. 4 Sept 17 Albany R.E.
    DAMA RAGO   DADA JOGI   Signal officer.
    PALI MALA   JUGY JOVA   Staff Captain

| Sender's Number. | Day of Month. | In reply to Number. | AAA |
| RM 242 | 18th | | |

In continuation RM349 aaa Ref Sheet 37 1/40.000 aaa JUZI will advance to line WILLEMS M.5.d - SAILY - LAMOY G.28.d aaa boundaries southern L20.d.o.o. R.5.a.0.0 - M.5.a.0.0 northern L 16.b.15. G 28.b.30.10. Inter Bn boundary L35 central - L35 central. aaa ROM! and DAMA will march covered by screen of troops having to take up above line aaa mounted officers should be sent on to reconnoitre the route aaa Bns will not pass the line L.23.a - R.5.a before 1000 aaa Bde H.Q. will close at 1030 and open at FOREST VILLE on arrival aaa A report centre will be established at road junction L33.d.5.80. at 1030 until opening of new H.Q. where all messages will be sent aaa Pali will hold new line LM.45 defence East of Rly. Rt flank L.20.d.0.0. Lft flank L.80.0.0. bag distribution as per RM349 18th aaa acknowledge.

The above may be forwarded as now corrected. (Z)
JUZI.
    Censor.   Signature of Addressor or person authorised to telegraph in his name.

* This line should be erased if not required.

25th "King's" (Liverpool Regt.)

    The Brigadier wishes to congratulate and thank O.C. and all other ranks 25th Battn. "The King's" (Liverpool Regt.) on their wonderful performance during the recent advance.
    The Battalion has covered 30 miles in 36 hours in order to get into action.
    He especially wishes to express his appreciation of the spirit a of determination to get forward displayed, which has surmounted apparently insuperable obstacles and has resulted in the Battalion being the first British troops to cross the ESCAULT as a tactical unit.

                                      (Sd.) L.B.BRIERLEY,
                                                    Capt.
                                            A/Brigade Major.
21..10..18.   176th Infantry Brigade

CIRCULATION SLIP.

GENERAL STAFF (O) FIFTH ARMY.

No. SA 490/14   Date 24/10/18

- Army Commander
- M.G.G.S.
- G.S.O. 1 (a)
- G. (b)
- G. (c)
- G. (t)
- G.S.O. 3 (a)
- M.G.
- G. (i)
- A.
- Q.
- D.D.S. & T.
- D.D.O.S.
- G.O.C.R.A.
- C.E.
- C. of M.
- D.D. Signals
- D.M.S.
- P.M.
- R.A.F.
- C.A.
- French Liaison
- A.A.D.C.
- A.D.G.T.

Initials of Officer for filing ....

Printed in France by A.P. & S.S.   Press B. 2223a. 5000. 6-18.

Fifth Army,
G.A. 490/14.
25th Oct., 1918.

XI Corps. (2).
───────────

    I am to request you to convey to the 25th Bn King's Liverpool Regt. the Army Commander's appreciation of the dash and determination shewn by that Battalion during its advance on October 18th., 19th., 20th. and 21st., and his appreciation also of its endurance and gallantry which reflect great credit on all ranks.

                                               Major-General, G.S.

XI Corps G.S.67/37.

Fifth Army.

> H.Q., FIFTH ARMY,
> GENERAL STAFF.
> (O) 1800
> No. GA.490/14
> Date 24-10-18

Forwarded.

I think the Army Commander would be interested to read this report of the energy and determination shown during the recent advance by the 25th Bn. King's Liverpool Regt.

R. Haking

XI Corps.
23/10/18.

Lieut. General,
Commanding XI Corps.

XI Corps

G.871.

I give an account below of the operations carried out by the 25th Bn. King's Liverpool Regt.

The 25th Bn. King's Liverpool Regt. marched from FM du BIEZ, CHAPELLE d'ARMENTIERES at dawn on October 18th and reached ST.ANDRE at 1-0 p.m. The Battalion continued the march to WASQUEHAL reaching there at 6-0 p.m.

At dawn on October 19th the march was continued to HEM, where the Battalion passed through the 26th Bn. Royal Welch Fusiliers, and became part of the Advanced Guard. It reached HULANS at 3-0 p.m., advancing in artillery formation across country, covering a total distance of 30 miles in 33 hours.

On October 20th the Battalion continued the advance and reached West Bank of L'ESCAUT.

On October 21st by 5-0 p.m. 1½ Companies had crossed the river by pontoon in face of enemy resistance from Machine Guns and Trench Mortars.

22nd Oct.1918.

Major-General,
Commanding 59th Division.

Army Form C. 2118.

WAR DIARY
or
INTELLIGENCE SUMMARY.
(Erase heading not required.)

Confidential.

Original.

War Diary
of
25th Bn. "The King's" (Liverpool Regiment)

From :- 1st Novr. 1918.
To :- 30th Novr. 1918.

Army Form C. 2118.

WAR DIARY
or
INTELLIGENCE SUMMARY. 25th Pavilings (Pool Regt)

(Erase heading not required.)

Instructions regarding War Diaries and Intelligence Summaries are contained in F.S. Regs., Part II. and the Staff Manual respectively. Title pages will be prepared in manuscript.

Place	Date	Hour	Summary of Events and Information	Remarks and references to Appendices
TOUFFLERS	1-11-18		Weather fine. Casualties nil. Bn carried out a tactical scheme.	HSN
	2-11-18		Weather showery. Casualties nil. Bn. training	HSN
	3-11-18		Weather fine. Casualties nil. Church parade.	HSN
	4-11-18		Weather fine. Casualties nil. Bn training	HSN
	5-11-18		Weather fine. Casualties nil. Bn training. Orders received to prepare to be ready to move forward at 1 hours notice from 09.45 hours. LT.W.J.ROBSON M.C. joined the Bn, having posted from 36B/Northumberland Fusiliers	HSN
	6-11-18		Weather fine. Casualties nil. Bn training. The following N.C.Os & men were awarded the Mily (?) Medal for Gallantry in the field. No 204724 Sergt W. ECKERSLEY, No 106051 Cpl J.T. MELLOR, No 381983 L/Cpl L. HARRIS, No 381962 L/Cpl R.A.S. HUNT and No 381931 Pte R. DENLEY Authority D.R.O 1780 dated 5-11-18.	HSN
	7-11-18	10.30	Weather fine. Casualties nil. Bn training. Orders received to move the following day. (Marked A)	HSN
	8-11-18	12.00	Weather fine. Casualties nil. Orders received to move. (marked B)	HSN

Army Form C. 2118.

WAR DIARY
or
INTELLIGENCE SUMMARY.   25th Bn/Rags Royal Regt.

(Erase heading not required.)

Place	Date	Hour	Summary of Events and Information	Remarks and references to Appendices
TOUFFLERS	8-11-18	15.00	Bn moved off.	HQ
CHAOS		16.00	Bn arrived at CHAOS and went into Billets	HQ
			Capt. J.A. DICKENSON awarded military cross. Authority D.R.O. 1785 dated 8-11-18	HQ
"	9-11-18		Orders received to be ready to move in the morning on receiving the code word MOVE.	HQ
			Weather fine. Casualties nil.	HQ
		09.45	Message received MOVE. at 10.15.	HQ
		10.15	Bn moved off	HQ
		12.00	Arrived [HQ] on west bank of river ESCAULT (SCHELDT). Bn had dinner.	HQ
		13.00	Bn moved off, crossed pontoon bridge and marched to GOUDINIERE	HQ
GOUDINIERE		19.00	Arrived in billets.	HQ
			Orders received to move at 07.00 hours in the morning.	HQ
			Weather fine and very cold. Casualties nil.	HQ
"	10-11-18	07.00	Bn moved off	HQ
VELAINES		10.00	Bn arrived at VELAINES.	HQ
"		12.00	Orders received to move to FOREST.	HQ
		13.00	Orders broken and Bn kept Cancelled and Bn billeted in VELAINES.	HQ

Army Form C. 2118.

WAR DIARY
or
INTELLIGENCE SUMMARY.

2 5th Bn Rifle Brgd Sport Bn.

(Erase heading not required.)

Place	Date	Hour	Summary of Events and Information	Remarks and references to Appendices
VELAINES	10-11-18		Bn billeted. HQ in CHATEAU	
	11-11-18	11.15	Wire received. Hostilities will cease at 11.00 to day	
		12.00	Bn paraded in Chateau grounds and store keepers read out Warning order received to be ready on receipt of message "NONE" to move off in accordance with march table attached marked "D".	
		23.15	ALL message MOVE	
	12-11-18	09.00	Bn moved off	
GOUDINIERE		11.30	Bn arrived at GOUDINIERE Weather fine but wet. Casualties nil	
"	13-11-18		Weather fine. Bn resting & cleaning up.	
	14-11-18		Bn training. Weather fine Orders received to move to WILLEMS the following day marked "E"	
	15-11-18	10.26	Bn moved off	
		16.00	Bn arrived at WILLEMS and went into billets	
WILLEMS	16-11-18	11.07	Orders received to move at 11.00 hours to THUMESNIL (LILLE) Bn moved off.	
		15.30	Bn arrived at THUMESNIL and went into billets.	
THUMESNIL	17-11-18		Bn Voluntary Church parade	

Army Form C. 2118.

WAR DIARY
or
INTELLIGENCE SUMMARY. 28th Bn Kings (Liverpool) Regt.

(Erase heading not required.)

Place	Date	Hour	Summary of Events and Information	Remarks and references to Appendices
THUMESNIL	18-11-16		Bn training. 1 O.R. died in hospital from broncho pneumonia.	AAA
	19-11-16		Bn training. The following officers were awarded the Military Cross for gallantry in the field 2/Lt L. STAGG, 2/Lt E. SAYER & 2/Lt G. PHIPPS and also No 381 Sgt Cpl. M. WEED was awarded the D.C.M. for bravery in the field. Authority DRO 1820 dated 19-11-16	AAA AAA AAA
	20-11-16		Bn training. Lt. H.A.H. WALKER awarded Military Cross & brevity in the field. Authority DRO 1825 dated 20-11-16.	AAA
	21-11-16		Weather fine. Bn training	AAA
	22-11-16		Weather fine. Bn training	AAA
	23-11-16		Weather fine. No Bn training. All attended Bde Gymkhana.	AAA
	24-11-16		Weather fine. Bde. Church Parade. and the following officers and ORs were presented with medal ribands (with they had been awarded) by Major General N.M. Smyth V.C.C.B. Commanding 59th Division. Capt J.H. DICKENSON, 2/Lt E. SAYER, Sergt W. WRAGG, Sergt W. WOOD, Cpl. M. WEED and 2/Lt L. HARRIS	AAA

Army Form C. 2118.

WAR DIARY
or
INTELLIGENCE SUMMARY.   25th Bn Kings (Liverpool) Regt

(Erase heading not required.)

Place	Date	Hour	Summary of Events and Information	Remarks and references to Appendices
THAMESHILL	25-11-18		Weather fine. Bn training	A/W
	26-11-18		Weather fine. Bn training. Education classes have started	A/W
	27-11-18		Weather fine. Bn training	A/W
	28-11-18		Weather wet. 2/Lt J.S. LANDER, 2/Lt A.L. BRAMWELL, 2/Lt T.H. LANGRIDGE, 2/Lt J.R.S. BRIGGS, 2/Lt F.A. SANDERS, 2/Lt A.E. LAWTON joined Bn	A/W
	29-11-18		Weather wet. Bn training and education classes.	A/W
	30-11-18		Weather fine. " " " " " " "	A/W
			N/M SMYTH V.C. C.B. inspected the transport.	A/W

Chas Hand
MAJOR
Commanding 25 BN. THE KINGS (LIVERPOOL REGT)

Army Form C. 2118.

WAR DIARY
or
INTELLIGENCE SUMMARY.
(Erase heading not required.)

Instructions regarding War Diaries and Intelligence Summaries are contained in F. S. Regs., Part II. and the Staff Manual respectively. Title pages will be prepared in manuscript.

Confidential.

Original.

War Diary.

25th Bn "The King's" (Liverpool Regiment)

From: Decr 1st 1918.
To: Decr 31st 1918.

Army Form C. 2118.

WAR DIARY
or
INTELLIGENCE SUMMARY. 25th Bn the "King's" Liverpool Regt

(Erase heading not required.)

Place	Date	Hour	Summary of Events and Information	Remarks and references to Appendices
TAHMESNIL	1-12-18		A draft of the undermentioned Jnr officers Lt. J.W.A. MANN, W.G. OLDFIELD, M.M., G.L. COOKE & W. SMITH and 53 other ranks arrived.	ACM
"	2-12-18		Bn. war training, attended military and educational. Lt. R.F. GWYNN and 2/Lt. TORMEROD rejoined Bn. from hospital	ACM
"	3-12-18		Training, military & educational. Sent out warning orders to move.	ACM
	4-12-18		Training, military & educational.	ACM
	5-12-18		Training. Issued orders for Bn to move to VERDREL.	ACM
	6-12-18	10.30	Bn entrained	ACM
VERDREL		15.30	" arrived at VERDREL and was billetted in huts	ACM
	7-12-18		Day spent in preparing camp	ACM
	8-12-18		Sunday. Church Parade	ACM
	9-12-18		Training military & educational	ACM
	10-12-18		"	ACM
	11-12-18		"	ACM
	12-12-18		No training. A draft of 56 o.Rs arrived at about 22.00 hours.	ACM

Army Form C. 2118.

2/5th Bn "The King's" Liverpool Regt

WAR DIARY
INTELLIGENCE SUMMARY.
(Erase heading not required.)

Instructions regarding War Diaries and Intelligence Summaries are contained in F. S. Regs., Part II. and the Staff Manual respectively. Title pages will be prepared in manuscript.

Place	Date	Hour	Summary of Events and Information	Remarks and references to Appendices
VERDREL	13.12.18		Training, military & Educational	App
"	14.12.18		" " "	App
"	15.12.18		Received & issued orders to move to BARLIN. Sunday. Church Parade	App
	16.12.18	9.30	'B' Co moved off.	App
BARLIN		11.0	'B' arrived. Billeted in huts & schools.	App
	17.12.18		Day spent improving billets	App
	18.12.18		Training, military & educational	App
	19.12.18		Section in training. Bn cross country run.	App
	20.12.18		Training, military & educational.	App
	21.12.18		" " "	App
	22.12.18		Sunday Church parade.	App
	23.12.18		Been Training, military & educational	App
	24.12.18		" " "	App
	25.12.18		Christmas Day.	App
	26.12.18		No training. Bn Paper Chase	App

WAR DIARY
or
INTELLIGENCE SUMMARY.

25th Bn The King's "Liverpool Regt"

Army Form C. 2118.

Place	Date	Hour	Summary of Events and Information	Remarks and references to Appendices
BARLIN	27-12-18		Training military & educational	
	28-12-18		" "	
	29-12-18		Sunday Church Parade	
		10.25	Rec'd order Bn prepare to move at short notice	
	30-12-18		Training military & educational	
		10.00	Orders above suspended	
	31-12-18		Training military & educational	
	1-1-19			

L. E. Lambelle Lieut-Colonel
Comm'd 25th Bn King's Liverpool Regt

BM/144.
5/12/18.

Kings L'pool Regt.
R.Welch Fus.
R.Sussex Regt.
176 C.O.M. Bty.
467 Field Coy RE
2/1st Fd. Amb.

Instructions for embussing 6/12/18.

1. Brigade Order No. 144 para 2 is cancelled. Units will embus in following order from the front:-
   Div HQ Group
   R.Sussex Regt.
   R.Welch Fus.
   Kings L'pool Regt.
   Bde HQ.
   L.T.M.B.
   467 Fd. Coy RE
   2/1st (NM) Fd. Amb.

2. Div HQ Group, R.Sussex Regt. and part of R.Welch Fus. will embus in 58 buses which are drawn up on right of the LILLE – WATTIGNIES Road, the head at X Roads Q.26.d.0.9.
   The remainder of Welch and rest of Bde Group will embus in the column

of lorries which will be drawn up on the right of the same road with head at G.21.a.0.0.

3. Markers and guides will meet the Brigade Major at Bde HQ at 0815 as under :-

King's L'pool Regt		2 OR.
R Welch Fus	1 officer	4 OR.
R Sussex	1 officer	3 OR.
L.T.M.B.		1 OR.
467 Fd Coy RE		2 OR.
2/1st W.M. Fd Amb		2 OR.

4. Markers will be posted at the front and rear lorry to be occupied by each unit. Troops will be marched on to these markers at 0920 and embus forthwith.

5. (i) The officer of the RWF will be informed of the number of lorries available for his Bn. in the front and rear convoys respectively and will return to Bn HQ with this information.

(ii) One lorry next to Bde HQ lorry will be allotted to the Sussex for carrying their cooking utensils and 8 men. A marker will be posted at this lorry and the officer shown where it is in order that he may guide the carrying party.

③

6. There will be a halt of 10 minutes the hours from the time the convoy starts when men may fall out.

7. <u>Debussing</u> Attached wire B.M. n=0 gives debussing arrangements. Troops will fall out on the right of the road until lorry convoy moves on, and units will then be led by guides to their Camps.

8. <u>Acknowledge</u>.

P.M Mansergh

Captain a/Brig Major
176° Infantry Bde.

5/12/18.

"A" Form.
MESSAGES AND SIGNALS.

Army Form C.2121
(in pads of 100.)
No. of Message _____

| Prefix ___ Code ___ m. | Words | Charge | This message is on a/c of : | Recd. at ___ m. |
| Office of Origin and Service Instructions. | Sent At ___ m. To By | | _____ Service. (Signature of "Franking Officer.") | Date ___ From ___ By |

TO Lt Maynard c/o Signals BARLIN

| Sender's Number. | Day of Month. | In reply to Number. | AAA |
| * OM100 | 5 | | |

Ra party due to arrive
1300 hrs tomorrow aaa
@ detraining point on HALLICOURT -
BARLIN Road head at X roads
K20 c 1.2 aaa Raes in column
Sussex W.R.Rifles Liverpools Bde HQ L.T.M.B.
Field Coy Field Amb aaa
Have 2/ guides per unit
at detraining point aaa
Limbers of Liverpools and Sussex
to be at Bde. H.Q.
ready to carry overs etc
to camp aaa acknowledge

From 176 Inf Bde
Place
Time

The above may be forwarded as now corrected. (Z)
Censor. Signature of Addressor or person authorised to telegraph in his name.
* This line should be erased if not required.

SECRET.

176th INFANTRY BRIGADE ORDER NO.144.

COPY NO. 1.

4.12.13.

Ref: 1/40,000 Map.
Sheets 36 and 44 B.

1. The Dismounted personnel of the Brigade Group will proceed by Bus from FROIDURE to the BARLIN area on the 6th December embussing on the road between Q.26.d.0.9. and Q.15.c.4.0. facing South, at 0930 hours.

2. Units will embus in the following order from the front :-

   Divl. H.Q. Group.(under O.C. 250th Divl.Emp.Coy).
   Royal Welsh Fusrs.
   King's L'pool Regt.
   Royal Sussex Regt.
   467 Fd.Coy. R.E.
   2/1st (N.M.) F.Amb.
   176th Bde.H.Q., Signal Section,
   and L.T.M.Battery.

   Troops will be at Embussing Point by 0920 hours.

3. Troops will be told off into groups of 25 all ranks for purposes of Embussing.

4. Detailed instructions as to how embussing is to be carried out and instructions as to Debussing will be issued later. Debussing points will be either at Unit Camps or close to BARLIN. In latter case Bde.Advance Party will provide guides.

5. Motor Ambulances are to move as a Convoy under the orders of the A.D.M.S.

6. Locations of Camps in the new area will be as follows :-

   Brigade H.Qrs.   K.27.c.25.05.   Sheet 44 B.
   25th K.L'pool Regt.   Q.14.d.9.9.
   26th R.Welch Fusrs.   K.26.b.2.2.
   17th R.Sussex Regt.   J.36.c.2.2.
   176th L.T.M.Battery.   K.27.c.1.1.
   2/1st (N.M.) F.Amb.   K.33.a.7.7.
   467 Fd.Coy. R.E.   K.33.b.3.9.
   No.2 Coy. Div.Train.   K.33.b.3.9.

7. <u>Supply arrangements</u> during move are as follows :-

   Double refill on 4th inst.
   Rations for consumption 6th inst. will be carried on the man.
   Rations for consumption 7th inst. will be drawn from Supply Refilling Point at K.27.a.1.3. at 15.30 hours on 6th inst.
   The Officer i/c Advanced Parties of all units has been ordered to send a representative to that point to guide supply wagons to Qr.Mr.Stores.

(2).

8. Personnel will carry packs, and one blanket.
Necessary dixies kept behind for cooking after the departure of transport will also be taken on personnel busses.

9. <u>Lorries for second blanket.</u>   Lorries will report at Brigade Headquarters at 0800 hours on the 6th inst. for carriage of second blanket, as follows :-

25th K.L'pool Regt.	2 Lorries.
26th R.Welch Fusrs.	2 Lorries.
17th R.Sussex Regt.	1 Lorry.
176th Bde.H.Qrs.) 176th L.T.M.Bty.)	1 lorry.

The above Units must send a guide to Brigade Headquarters at 0800 hours to guide these lorries to where required. After loading up they will return to Brigade Headquarters and proceed to the new area in one convoy.
The 25th King's Liverpool Regt. will detail an officer to take charge of this convoy.

10. Leave Train in the new area departs LAPUGNOY at 1353 hours on day prior to commencement of leave.

11. Brigade Headquarters will close at FROIDURE at 0830 hours 6th Decr. and reopen at K.27.c.25.05. on arrival.

12. ACKNOWLEDGE.

Issued at 1600 hours
through Signals.

JG Shorter
for
Captain. a/Brigade Major.
176th Infantry Brigade.

Distribution :-

Copy No. 1 K.L'pool Regt.
        2. R.Welch Fusrs.
        3. R.Sussex Regt.
        4. 176th L.T.M.Bty.
        5. G.O.C.
        6. Brigade Major.
        7. Staff Captain.
        8. Brigade Transport Officer.
        9. Signals.
       10. 467th Fd.Coy. R.E.
       11. 2/1st (N.M.)F.Amb.
       12. No.2 Coy. Div.Train.
       13. File.
       14.)
       15) War Diary.

Army Form C. 2118.

WAR DIARY
or
INTELLIGENCE SUMMARY.
(Erase heading not required.)

Confidential

Original

War Diary of

25" Bn "The King's (Liverpool Regiment)

January 1" - July 31" 1918

WAR DIARY

Army Form C. 2118.

INTELLIGENCE SUMMARY. 25th Bn The Kings Liverpool Regt

(Erase heading not required.)

Place	Date	Hour	Summary of Events and Information	Remarks and references to Appendices
BARLIN	1-1-19		Austrian Routes Gazette Lt Col C.E. LEMBCKE, D.S.O., promotion to Brevet Major & Mentioned and A/Lt No. 110 A/87 L/Cpl TICKLE. R.M.M. mentioned. 1 Time Serving Soldier sent to Base.	AKA
	2-1-19		Bn having military & Educational Training	AKA
	3-1-19		Bn recreational training. Men sent home for demobilization.	AKA
			Bn training military & Educational. Two men sent to demobilization.	AKA
			Orders received to move to WALLON CAPEL on 7th Jan. (orders attached)	AKA
	4-1-19		Bn training military & educational. Three O.R. sent to demobilization.	AKA
	5-1-19		Sunday. Church parades.	AKA
	6-1-19		Bn training military & educational. Advance party went 1st VENANT.	AKA
			Orders received in the evening that move to motor transport. Postponed.	AKA
	7-1-19		Bn training military & educational. Advance party brought back from ST VENANT	AKA
	8-1-19		Bn training military & educational	AKA
	9-1-19		Bn recreational training	AKA
	10-1-19		Bn training military & Educational. Lt J.H.M. SHIER & 4 O.R.'s went for demobilization.	AKA
	11-1-19		Bn training military & educational. 6 O.R's sent for demobilization. Message received that the Colours would be presented to the Bn on parade on 14th by Bde.	AKA

Army Form C. 2118.

WAR DIARY
or
INTELLIGENCE SUMMARY.
(Erase heading not required.)

25th Bn Kings Liverpool Regt

Instructions regarding War Diaries and Intelligence Summaries are contained in F. S. Regs., Part II. and the Staff Manual respectively. Title pages will be prepared in manuscript.

Place	Date	Hour	Summary of Events and Information	Remarks and references to Appendices
BARLIN	12-1-19		Church parade. Orders received the Colours would be presented next Sat.	
			of 18th Inf Bde but moved to be presented on 14-1-19 as a Bn parade.	
			There are 108 men engaged under home on leave + 2 off. sent for demobilization	
	13-1-19		Rehearsal parade for presentation of Colours ceremony. 10 OR	
			sent for demobilization.	
	14-1-19		Colours presented to the Bn. by Major General D.M.SMYTH.V.C., C.B.	
			A copy of the proceedings & speech is attached. 10 ORs sent for	
			demobilization. Orders received to move to WALLON CAPEL on 16th	
	16-1-19		Orders issued for move, advance party went to ST VENANT and Bn	
			prepared to move.	
	16-1-19	9·00	Bn moved off.	
ST. VENANT		15·10	Bn arrived ST VENANT and billeted for the night.	
	17-1-19	9·00	Bn moved off.	
WALLON CAPEL		12·50	Arrived WALLON CAPEL. Bn in billets.	
	18-1-19		Bn training, military & educational.	
	19-1-19		Church parade.	

WAR DIARY
or
INTELLIGENCE SUMMARY. 25th Bn The King's Liverpool Regt.

Army Form C. 2118.

(Erase heading not required.)

Place	Date	Hour	Summary of Events and Information	Remarks and references to Appendices
HALLON CAPPEL.	20-1-19		Bn training military & educational. Four OR's sent for demobilization.	AEM
	21-1-19		" " " " " Five OR's " " "	AEM
	22-2-19		" " " " " 2/Lt HEW J. LANDER + 9 OR's sent	AEM
	23-1-19		for demobilization. Bn training & educational	AEM
	24-1-19		Bn training military & educational	AEM
	25-1-19		Bn training military & educational. WOs received from 176 2nd Bde that Bn would move to DUNKIRK on 27th (attached) 7 OR's sent for demobilization.	AEM
	26-1-19		Church parade. 30 OR's sent for demobilization. Verbal message that move on 27th was postponed	AEM
	27-1-19		Bn training military & educational 34 OR's sent for demobilization. Wire from BGC warning that move would probably be on 30th (attached)	AEM
	28-1-19		Bn training military & educational and 32 OR's sent for demobilization. 2/Lts W.G OLDFIELD + T.D McLEOD Lt Colonel C.E.J EMBERG DSO	AEM

WAR DIARY

INTELLIGENCE SUMMARY. 25th Bn. The King's (Liverpool Regt)

Army Form C. 2118.

Place	Date	Hour	Summary of Events and Information	Remarks and references to Appendices
WATTOU	25.1.19		Handed over command of the Bn. to Major Clive HARDY D.S.O. and	
CASSEL			Proceeded to take up duty at the WAR OFFICE. We are from Bde HQrs.	
			Bn moved entrain at HONDEGHEM on 25th & shortly most of Bn (about)	
			Bn preparing house 27 OR's about to demobilyn.	
	29.1.19		Bn moved off. Left 2/Lt F.A. SANDERS 4 OR's behind who are being sent	
	30.1.19	9.45	off. Demobilgat at Febvin. 24 OR's on 1st Feb, 5 OR's on 2nd Feb &	
			2/Lt F.A. SANDERS & 15 OR's on 3rd Feb.	
DUNKIRK	15 p.m	16.07	Bn arrived in camp, accommodated in tents.	
	31.1.19	1530	Bn prepared to take over duties of staffing Demobilization Camp	
			Transport arrived having done the journey by road	

Clive Hardy Major
Comm'ng 25th Bn. The King's Liverpool Regt.

Army Form C. 2118.

WAR DIARY
or
INTELLIGENCE SUMMARY.
(Erase heading not required.)

AH 10

Confidential

Original

War Diary

for

February
1919

25th Battn. The Kings L'pool. Regt.

WAR DIARY
INTELLIGENCE SUMMARY
(Erase heading not required.)

Army Form C. 2118.

25?B The Kings (Liverpool) Regt

Place	Date	Hour	Summary of Events and Information	Remarks and references to Appendices
DUNKIRK	1-2-19		Bn was carrying out duties in connection with Demobilisation Camp. 24 O.R.'s sent for demobilisation.	AHW
	2-2-19		Bn is now No.4 Demob'gdn Camp. B Coy has Rd Camp Commandant and found all personnel necessary. A, C & D Coys found 10, 11 & 12 Wings respectively and found all staff personnel necessary. 5 O.R.s sent for demob'n.	AHW
	3-2-19		Bn staffing No.4 Demob Camp. 2/Lt E.A.SANDERS & 25 O.R's sent for demob.	AHW
	4-2-19	"	16 O.R's sent for demob.	AHW
	5-2-19	"	2/Lt T.H.IANBRIDGE & 15 O.R's sent for demob.	AHW
	6-2-19	"	Few O.R's sent for demobilisation	AHW
	7-2-19	"	Few O.R's sent for demobilisation	AHW
	8-2-19	"	Few O.R's sent for demobilisation	AHW
	9-2-19	"	Capt W.R.WYLIE and 9 O.R's sent for demob.	AHW
	10-2-19	"	Few O.R's sent for demobilisation	AHW
	11-2-19	"	Few O.R's sent for demobilisation	AHW
	12-2-19	"	2/Lt H.F.JONES & 9 O.R's sent for demobilisation	AHW
	13-2-19	"	Few O.R's sent for demobilisation	AHW

Army Form C. 2118.

25th Bn. The King's Liverpool Regt.

WAR DIARY
or
INTELLIGENCE SUMMARY.

(Erase heading not required.)

Instructions regarding War Diaries and Intelligence Summaries are contained in F. S. Regs., Part II. and the Staff Manual respectively. Title pages will be prepared in manuscript.

Place	Date	Hour	Summary of Events and Information	Remarks and references to Appendices
DUNKIRK	14·2·19		Bn. staffing No. 4 Demobilization Camp. Few ORs sent for demobilization	AEA
	15·2·19		" Capt J.A. DICKENSON M.C. & 90 ORs sent for demobilisation	AEA
			" Few ORs sent for demobilisat. Lt Colonel	AEA
	16·2·19		" Few ORs sent for demobilisat.	AEA
			G.H.M. RICHEY D.S.O. joined the Bn in the Field and took over command	AEA
	17·2·19		Bn. staffing No. 4 Demobilization Camp. Lt. W.G. LOFTHOUSE, J.F. WARRELL, H. IRWIN M.C.M.M., & H. CHESHIRE M.C., 2/Lts. R.W. FRANKLAND, T.H. AMER and 162 ORs joined the Bn in the Field and were taken on strength. Bn	AEA
			" sent a draft from the 8th Bn the King's Liverpool Regt. (Liverpool Irish)	AEA
			10 ORs sent for demobilisat.	AEA
	18·2·19		Bn. staffing No. 4 Demobilisat. Camp. Few ORs sent for demobilisat.	AEA
	19·2·19		" Few ORs sent for demobilisat.	AEA
	20·2·19		" "	AEA
	21·2·19		" Few ORs sent for demobilisation	AEA
			2/Lt. A.F. JONES then joined the Bn in the Field and was taken on strength. 8th Bn the King's	AEA
			Was a part of the draft from 8th Bn the King's	AEA
	22·2·19		Bn. staffing No. 4 Demobilisation camp. 17 ORs sent for Demob.	AEA

Army Form C. 2118.

WAR DIARY
or
INTELLIGENCE SUMMARY.
(Erase heading not required.)

23rd Bn the Kings Liverpool Regt

Instructions regarding War Diaries and Intelligence Summaries are contained in F. S. Regs., Part II. and the Staff Manual respectively. Title pages will be prepared in manuscript.

Place	Date	Hour	Summary of Events and Information	Remarks and references to Appendices
DUNKIRK	23.2.19		Bn staffing No 4 Demob. Camp. 19 ORs sent for demobilization	AHH
	24.2.19		" " " "	AHH
	25.2.19		" " " Two ORs sent for demobilization	AHH
	26.2.19		" " "	AHH
	27.2.19		" " " One OR sent for demobilization	AHH
	28.2.19		" " " Brigade orders (attached) ordering	AHH
			us to take over No 5 Demob camp on February 1st day	

G. Hunt Risley
Lt Colonel
Commg. 23rd Bn the Kings Liverpool Regt

1-3-19.

Army Form C. 2118.

WAR DIARY
or
INTELLIGENCE SUMMARY.
(Erase heading not required.)

Instructions regarding War Diaries and Intelligence Summaries are contained in F. S. Regs., Part II. and the Staff Manual respectively. Title pages will be prepared in manuscript.

Place	Date	Hour	Summary of Events and Information	Remarks and references to Appendices

Original

Confidential

War Diary
of
25ᵗʰ Kings Liverpool Regt

From March 1st 1919
To March 31st 1919

Army Form C. 2118.

WAR DIARY
or
INTELLIGENCE SUMMARY. 25th Bn. The King's Liverpool Regt

(Erase heading not required.)

Instructions regarding War Diaries and Intelligence Summaries are contained in F. S. Regs., Part II. and the Staff Manual respectively. Title pages will be prepared in manuscript.

Place	Date	Hour	Summary of Events and Information	Remarks and references to Appendices
DUNKIRK	1.3.19		Bn moved from No 14 to No 5 Demobilization Camp and took over the duty of staffing same. Six officers and 210 ORs joined the Bn being drafts from the 6th, 7th, 8th & 9th Bn King's Liverpool Regt. The names of the officers are Capt E.G.H. ROBERTS MC, Lt. H.J. SPARGO, Lt W. ROYDEN, Lt. SE.NICHOLAS Lt. G.H. LEAK Lt. D.J. WILLIAMS.	A/H
	2.3.19		Bn staffing No 5 Demob. Camp. R.S.M. FARQUHARSON demobilised.	A/H
	3.3.19		" " " " " "	A/H
	4.3.19		" " " " Three ORs demobilised.	A/H
	5.3.19		" " " " Capt. A.A. CARBERRY M.C. Liverpool Regt. joined the Bn.	A/H
	6.3.19		Joined the Bn.	A/H
	7.3.19		Bn staffing No 5. Demob. Camp. Lt. L.O. ATKINSON. Liverpool Regt. joined the Bn.	A/H
	8.3.19		" " " " Two ORs demobilised.	A/H
	9.3.19		" " " "	A/H
	10.3.19		" " " "	A/H
	11.3.19		" " " " Four officers & 124 ORs joined the Bn from the	A/H

WAR DIARY
or
INTELLIGENCE SUMMARY.

(Erase heading not required.)

Army Form C. 2118.

1st Bn. The King's Liverpool Regt

Place	Date	Hour	Summary of Events and Information	Remarks and references to Appendices
DUNKIRK	11.3.19		5th Bn. K.L.R. The officer being Lt. J.S. WILSON, Lt. J. HAYHURST, 2/Lt. E.W. BARKER	HCN
	12.3.19		Lt. C.V. OWEN	HCN
	12.3.19		Bn. staffing No. 5 Demob. Camp	HCN
	13.3.19		" " 100 joined the Bn. Reinforcement from 1/5 K.L.R.	HCN
	14.3.19		" "	HCN
	15.3.19		" " Lt. C.W. MORRISON Liverpool Regt. joined the Bn.	HCN
	16.3.19		" " 2nd Officer & 2 O.R. 1/6th K.L.R. joined the	HCN
			8th K.L.R.	HCN
	17.3.19		Bn. staffing being Lt. R.H. SPRIGINGS & Lt. VICTOR LEE.	HCN
	18.3.19		Bn. staffing No.5 Demob Camp. 160 Reinforcement from 8th K.L.R.	HCN
			8th K.L.R.	HCN
	19.3.19		" " HQrs " " 8th 1/5th K.L.R	HCN
	20.3.19		" " 2 O.R. " "	HCN
			2/Lts F. PAYNE & A.S. KEARTON sent for demobilyst-	HCN
			and 2 Lt. G.E. NICHOLAS transferred to 13th Bn. K.L.R.	HCN
	21.3.19		Bn. staffing No. 5 Demob Camp. 27 O.Rs reinforcements joined the Bn from 1/6 K.L.R.	HCN
	22.3.19		176 Inf. B to him No. SA. 13 reserves (Attacking)	HCN
			Balance of Coy will probably move to CALAIS on 24th inst. (Capt R. WILDE. D.S.O. MC)	HCN
			Just possibly formed the Bn.	

Army Form C. 2118.

WAR DIARY
or
INTELLIGENCE SUMMARY. 25th Bn. The Kings (Liverpool) Regt

(Erase heading not required.)

Place	Date	Hour	Summary of Events and Information	Remarks and references to Appendices
DUNKIRK	23.3.19		Bn Staffing No 6 Dismb Camp. 108 Reinforcement from 1/5th K.L.R. joined the Bn	
	24.3.19		" Three officer reinforcements from 9th K.L.R. being 2nd Lt A.R. HILL, 2nd Lt F.S.C. HOWE & 2nd Lt J.N. JARVIS. W/ee from 17 Bn BAC (attached). Bn less 1 Coy will move on to Calais	
	25.3.19		"	
	26.3.19		Bn Staffing No 5 Dismb Camp. 10 OR's from 1/6th KLR + 1 OR from 8th KLR reinforcements arrived	
	26.3.19		" Operation Order (attached) for move received.	
	27.3.19	07.55	Bn less "D" Coy moved to CALAIS by rail. Transport moved by road.	
		10.00	"A" Coy detrained at ZENEGHEM.	
		15.00	Bn less "A" & "D" Coys arrived CALAIS	
BEAUMARAIS		15.45	" arrived in No 3 Camp BEAUMARAIS. 87 O.R. reinforcements from 9th K.L.R. arrived and 9 O.R. reinforcements 1 Officer from 1/5th K.L.R. the officer being 2nd Lt EMERY.	
	28.3.19		Bn training. 4 officers and 150 OR reinforcement from 18th Lancashire Fusiliers arrived the officers being Capt. L.W. TOPHAM, 2nd Lt F. DAWSON 2nd Lt A.E.V. GALLON M.C., 2nd Lt T.C.A. HILL.	
	29.3.19		Bn moved to No 1 Camp BEAUMARAIS	

WAR DIARY
INTELLIGENCE SUMMARY

2/5th Bn. The King's (Liverpool Regt.)

Army Form C. 2118.

Place	Date	Hour	Summary of Events and Information	Remarks and references to Appendices
BEAUMARAIS	30.3.19		Bn. training. 42 ORs from 9th K.L.R., 96 ORs from 15th K.L.R. & 9 ORs from 16th K.L.R. reinforcement arrived.	Appx
	31.3.19		Bn training. 108 from 8th K.L.R. reinforcement arrived.	Appx
				Appx

G. M. Rainey Lt Col.
Commndg 2/5th Bn The King's Liverpool Regt.

31-3-19.

Army Form C. 2118.

WAR DIARY
or
INTELLIGENCE SUMMARY.
(Erase heading not required.)

Confidential

Originals

War Diary

of

25th Bn. Kings Liverpool Regt.

From :- 1st April 1919

To :- 30th April 1919

Army Form C. 2118.

WAR DIARY
or
INTELLIGENCE SUMMARY.
(Erase heading not required.)

2.5. A.B. 2/6 King's (Liverpool) Regt

Place	Date	Hour	Summary of Events and Information	Remarks and references to Appendices
BEAUMARAIS	1/9/19		Training. Capt E.G.H. ROBERTS M.C. posted to join 51st Bn. The King's Liverpool Regt. Lieut. WILDE S.O. M.C. took command O.D. Coy. Six (6) reinforcements from 1/6 Bn. King's Liverpool Regt. reinforced.	RS RS AS AS
"	2/9/19		Training. B. Coy moved to DIGUES DES ROMPUES to take over from guards. 2/Lt J. A. HUNTER + 1 O.R. joined the Bn. from 1/6 King's Liverpool Regt. C. Coy. moved to VALDELIEVRE to take over Ordnance guards. 14 O.Rs (reinforcements) joined from the 2/7 Bn. King's Liverpool Regt.	AS AS AS AS AS AS
"	3/9/19		4/Lt H. WILSON joined the Bn. from the 1/6 Bn. King's Liverpool Regt. 3 O.Rs (reinforcements) joined the Bn. from 1/6 King's Liverpool Regt.	AS AS
"	4/9/19		Sunday. Church Parades.	AS
"	5/9/19		The following reinforcements arrived. 1 O.R. from 2 MANCHESTER AS 9 O.Rs from 1/6 King's Liverpool Regt. & 4 O.Rs from the 2/7 King's Liverpool Regt.	AS AS

WAR DIARY or INTELLIGENCE SUMMARY

Army Form C. 2118.

25th King's (Liverpool Regt)

Place	Date	Hour	Summary of Events and Information	Remarks and references to Appendices
BEAUMORAIS	6/4/19		Miss. Y. CLARKE gave an Educational Lecture, subject— "The NEW WORLD".	AS
"	7/4/19		2/Lt. G.L. COOKE demobilised. 2 NCOs (reinforcements) joined from 11/s. King's Liverpool Regt.	AS
"	8/4/19		10 O.R's from 1/s King's Liverpool Regt joined the Bn.	AS
"	9/4/19		Duties. D.Coy. BATHS at DUNKIRK. C.Coy. Ordnance Guards at VAL DE LIÈVRE. B.Coy. Train Guards at DIGGES DES ROMAINS. A.Coy. Guards at ZENECHEM.	AS
"	"		Lt. H.M. WALKER M.C. + 2/Lt. E. LANE demobilised.	AS
"	13/4/19		2 O.R's joined the Bn. from 2/7 King's L.R. as reinforcements. One (1) reinforcement from 2/6 King's L.R. joined the Bn.	AS
"	14/4/19		Duties as per 9-4-19.	AS
"	13/4/19		Sunday Church Parades.	AS
"	"		2/6th K.L.R's joined the Bn. 6 O.R's (reinforcements) from	AS
"	14/4/19		Duties as per 9/4/19.	AS
"	15/4/19		" "	AS

WAR DIARY
or
INTELLIGENCE SUMMARY.

25th King's L.R.

Army Form C. 2118.

(Erase heading not required.)

Place	Date	Hour	Summary of Events and Information	Remarks and references to Appendices
BEAUMARAIS	16/4/19		Duties notes etc. in Batt. Guards & Town Guards.	R.S
"	17/4/19		Lt. D.D. RUTHERFORD M.C. joined the Bn; from the 18 Lancashire Fusiliers. 4 O.Rs (reinforcements) joined the Bn.	I.S
"			2/7 King's L.R.	I.S
"	18/4/19		Guard on Batt. Guards & Town Guards.	I.S
"	19/4/19		" "	I.S
"	20/4/19		Sunday. Church Parades. Inspection of Church Parade. by Brig. Genl. N.M. SMYTHE V.C.C.B.	I.S
"			O.C. "G" & "H" Coys. B. Coy. returned from Town Guard duty at DIEUES DES ROMAINS	R.S
"	21/4/19		30 O.Rs from 1/5 K.L.R joined the Bn.	R.S
"	22/4/19		20 O.Rs Demobilised.	I.S
"	23/4/19		Wire received from 76th Infantry Brigade, Battalion to select recent R.S.M. C.H.M RICHER D.S.O + officers + men to complete to 30 volunteer officers & 800 O.Rs for the EAST.	I.S

Army Form C. 2118.

WAR DIARY
or
INTELLIGENCE SUMMARY.

(Erase heading not required.)

2.S - 2st King's Liverpool Regt

Place	Date	Hour	Summary of Events and Information	Remarks and references to Appendices
BEDEHAVRES	24		A.C & D Coys rejoined the Bn. from Sewand & Bn Clubelies	CC
	25/4		Bn. Reviewed by MAJ. GEN N M SMYTHE VC CB, on Egypt.	CS
	25/4/19		Lt. J.S. ROOKLEDGE, 2/Lt. G.E. BRIGGS, 2/Lt. G. PHIPPS, 2/Lt. ISRAELFELD	CS
			Lft. Bn. for demobilisation.	CS
	26/4/19		Bn. Cleaning + organising for EAST.	CS
	27/4/19		Sunday Church Parades. 10% demobilised	CS
	28/4/19		Capt. R. HUTTON MC proceeded to Depot of Border Regt.	CS
			Capt. WM ROBSON MC demobilised	CS
	29/4/19		Medical Inspection of Bn for EAST. 40 O/Rs. joined enghit	CS
			S.O.R.S. demobilised. G.O.R.2 reinforcements joined Bn. from	CS
			9th Kings L.R.	CS
	30/4/19		Bn. training.	CS

C Staff eftch bh
L. Mgr Lt Col. Liverpool Regt.
Comdg 2.S - 2nd Kings

WAR DIARY
INTELLIGENCE SUMMARY
(Erase heading not required.)

Army Form C. 2118.

2/5th Bn. KING'S LIVERPOOL REGT.

Place	Date	Hour	Summary of Events and Information	Remarks and references to Appendices
BEAUMARAIS	1/5/19		Bn. still in CALAIS area. Orders arriving for the EAST	
	2/5/19		The following officers + 108 O.Rs. were Wounded in Depot & Duty H.C. HAWKINS, Capt. J.B. FOURNIER, RAMC (attached) 2/Lt. E.M. FRY	
	3/5/19		Wire received from H.Q. G.B.D. stating all officers + O.Rs. who had not had leave within 12 mths to proceed on leave 5-5-19 — 15-5-19	
	4/5/19		Sunday. Church Parades.	
	5/5/19 — 15/5/19		Bn. proceeded on leave U.K. via CALAIS.	
	17/5/19		Bn. returns from leave. Brigade R.H. RODDIE appointed as Q.M.	
	20/5/19		All officers + O.Rs. not proceeding to EAST attached to 1/5th K.R.R. CALAIS.	
	21/5/19		Bn. entrains at CALAIS for MARSEILLES. Strength 31 Officers + 665 O.Rs.	
en route	22/5/19		In Train.	
In PROVENCE	23/5/19		Train stopped at ST. GERMAINE. Bn. marched to overnight camp	

Army Form C. 2118.

WAR DIARY
or
INTELLIGENCE SUMMARY. 2s/4 B. The Kings Liverpool Regt
(Erase heading not required.)

Instructions regarding War Diaries and Intelligence Summaries are contained in F. S. Regs., Part II. and the Staff Manual respectively. Title pages will be prepared in manuscript.

Place	Date	Hour	Summary of Events and Information	Remarks and references to Appendices
St GERMAINE	23/5/15		where baths & refitment were supplied	
MARSEILLES	24/5/15/19		Bn. arrived at MARSEILLES & were accommodated at CARIS Rest Camp	
"	25/5/15		Bn equipped with drill clothing	
"	26/5/15		Preliminary orders for embarkation received	
"	29/5/15			
"	26/5/15		Bn. proceed through docks	
"			Bn. embarked on H.T. MALWA for EGYPT	
H.T. MALWA	29.5.15		Afloat MEDITERRANEAN SEA	
"	30.5.15			
"	31.5.15			
Port Said	2-6-15			

R.H. Delevoy Lt Col
Comdg. 2s/4 Kings Liverpool Regt

www.ingramcontent.com/pod-product-compliance
Lightning Source LLC
Chambersburg PA
CBHW081435160426
43193CB00013B/2288